© OperationReprint All Rights Reserved No part of this book may be reproduced or transmitted in any for or by any means; electronic or mechanical, including photocopying, scanner, recording or by information storage and retrieval system , without permission in writing from the publisher except for the review for inclusion in a magazine, newspaper or broadcast.

PLANISPHAERIVM SIVE MVNDI TOTIVS TYCHONIS PLANO

SCENO
SYSTEMATIS
PTOLE
GRAPHIA
MVNDANI
MAICI.
SEPTE NTRIO
MERI DIES
ORIENS
OCCIDENS
POLVS ARCTICVS
CIRCVLVS ARCTICVS
AXIS ZODIACI
TIORVM AXIS COLVRVS
TROPICVS ÆSTIVVS SEV TROPICVS CANCRI.
ÆQVATOR SEV ÆQVINOCTIALIS
ÆQVINOCTIALIS
SATVRNVS
IVPITER
SOL
MARS
LVNA
VENVS
MERCVRIVS
MAR DI
INDIA
Capricorni
TROPICVS HYBERNVS SIVE TROPICVS CAPRICORNI
SOLSTITIORVM MVNDI RVS
CIRCVLVS ANTARCTICVS.
POLVS ANTARCTICVS.
MERIDIANVS

SCENO
SYSTEMATIS
PTOLE
GRAPHIA
MVNDANI
MAICI.
SEPTE NTRIO
MERI DIES
OCCIDENS
ORIENS
POLVS ARCTICVS
CIRCVLVS ARCTICVS
POLVS ANTARCTICVS
CIRCVLVS ANTARCTICVS
TROPICVS ÆSTIVUS SEV TROPICVS CANCRI.
TROPICVS HYBERNVS SIVE TROPICVS CAPRICORNI
AXIS ZODIACI
AXIS MVNDI
COLVRVS SOLSTITIORVM
COLVRVS ÆQVINOCTIALIS
ÆQVATOR SEV ÆQVINOCTIALIS
MERIDIANVS
SATVRNVS
IVPITER
MARS
SOL
VENVS
MERCVRIVS
LVNA
INDIA
MAR DI

HÆMISPHÆ
LATUM AU
SPHÆRARUM
RIUM STEL
STRALE ÆQUALI
PROPORTIONE
VIRGO
LIBRA
SCORPIO
AQUARIUS

HEMISPHÆ
LATUM AU
SPHÆRARUM

RIUM STEL
STRALE ÆQUALI
PROPORTIONE

HÆMISPHÆRI
VM BOREALE
HÆMISPHÆRIO
UM STELLAT
CVM SUBIECTO
TERRESTRI.

HÆMISPHÆR
VM BOREALE
HÆMISPHÆRIO
UM STELLAT
CVM SUBIECTO
TERRESTRI.

HÆMISPHÆ
LATUM BO
ANTI
RIUM STEL
REALE
QVUM.
SCORPIO
LIBRA
VIRGO
SAGITTARIVS
AQVARIVS
Serpentarius
Aquila
Equuleus
Delphinus
Lyra
Cygnus
Pegasus
Draco
Bootes
Corvus
Andromeda
Cepheus
ARIES
Perseus
TAVRVS
GEMINI
CANCER
Auriga

HÆMISPHA
LATUM BO
ANTI
PISCES
AQVARIUS
Pegasus
Andromeda
Cepheus
Cygnus
Delphinus
Equuleus
Aquila
Lyra
SAGITTARIUS
Solstitiorum
Serpentarius
Serpens
Draco
Bootes
Corona
SCORPIO
LIBRA
VIRGO
Corvus
CANCER
GEMINI
Auriga
Perseus
TAURUS
Æquinoctiorum
TUM STEL
REALE
QVUM.

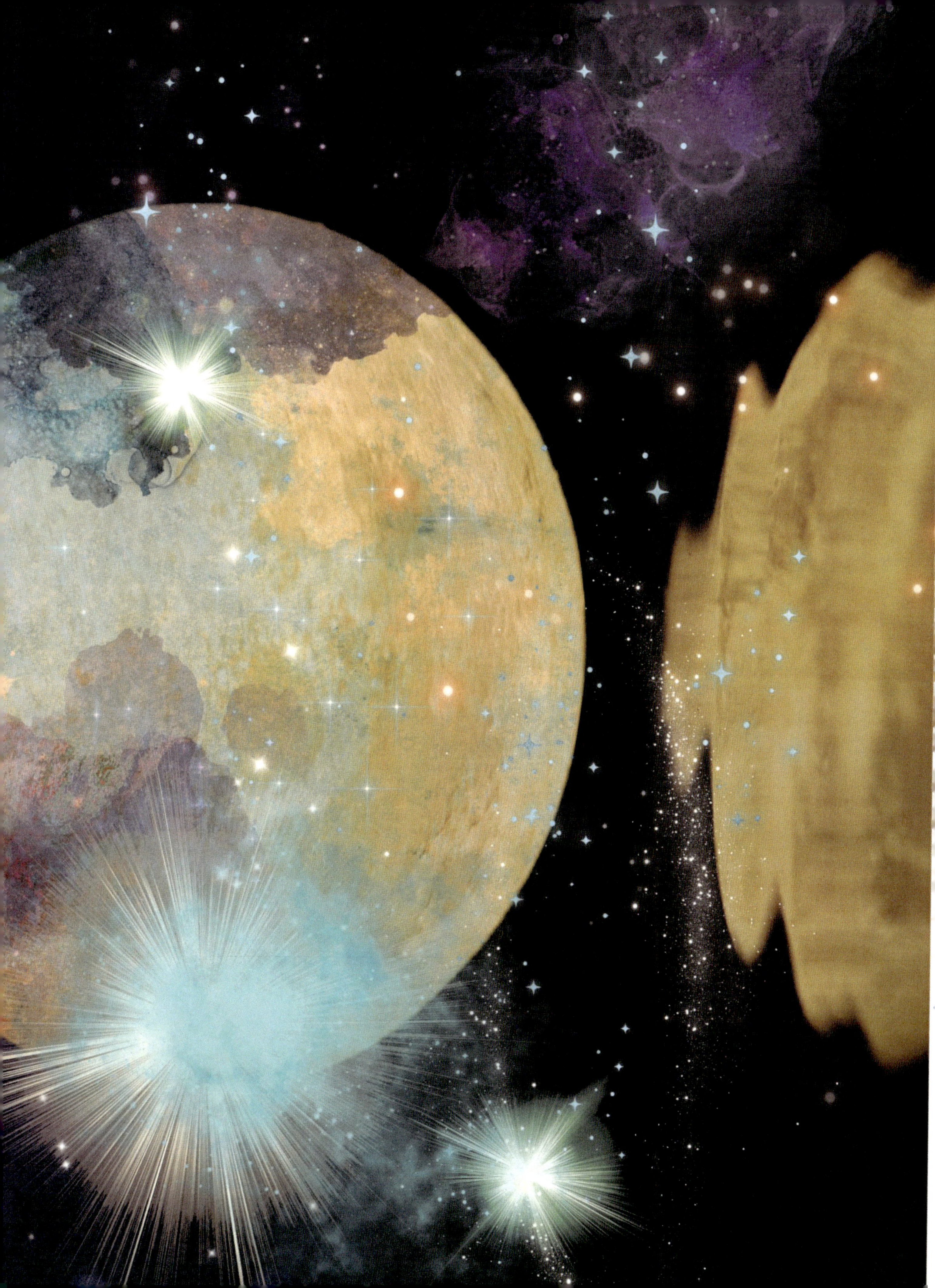

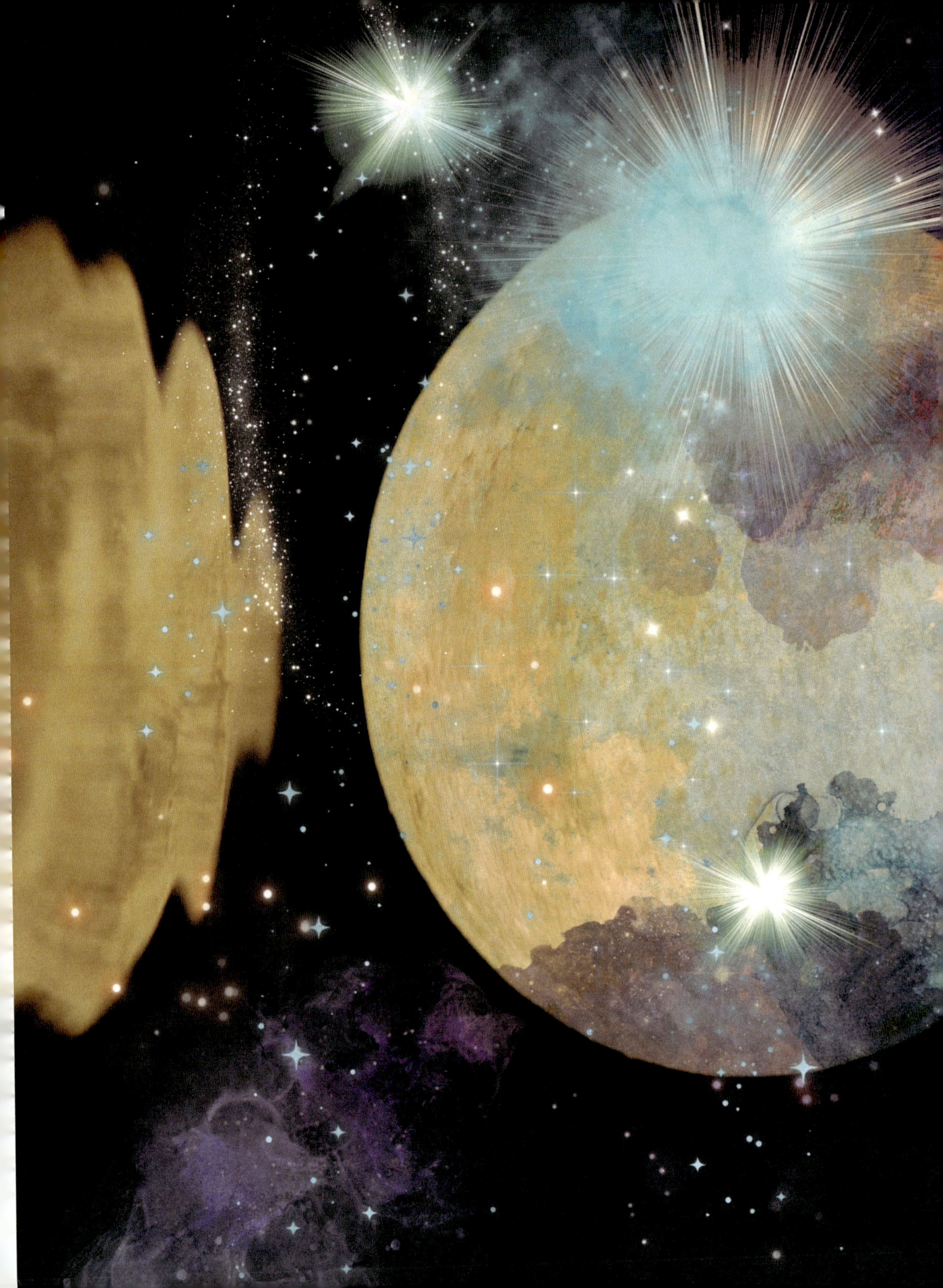

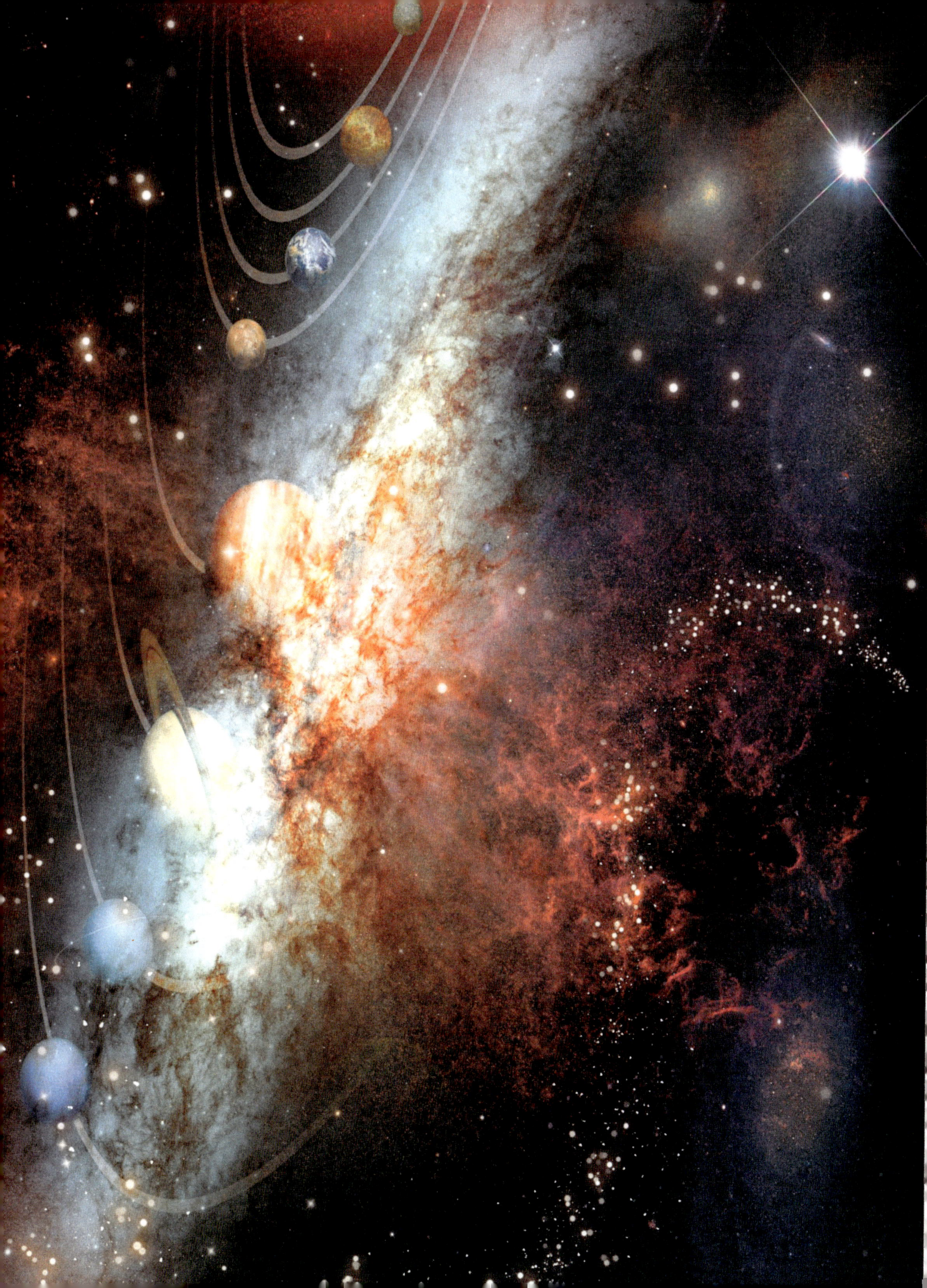

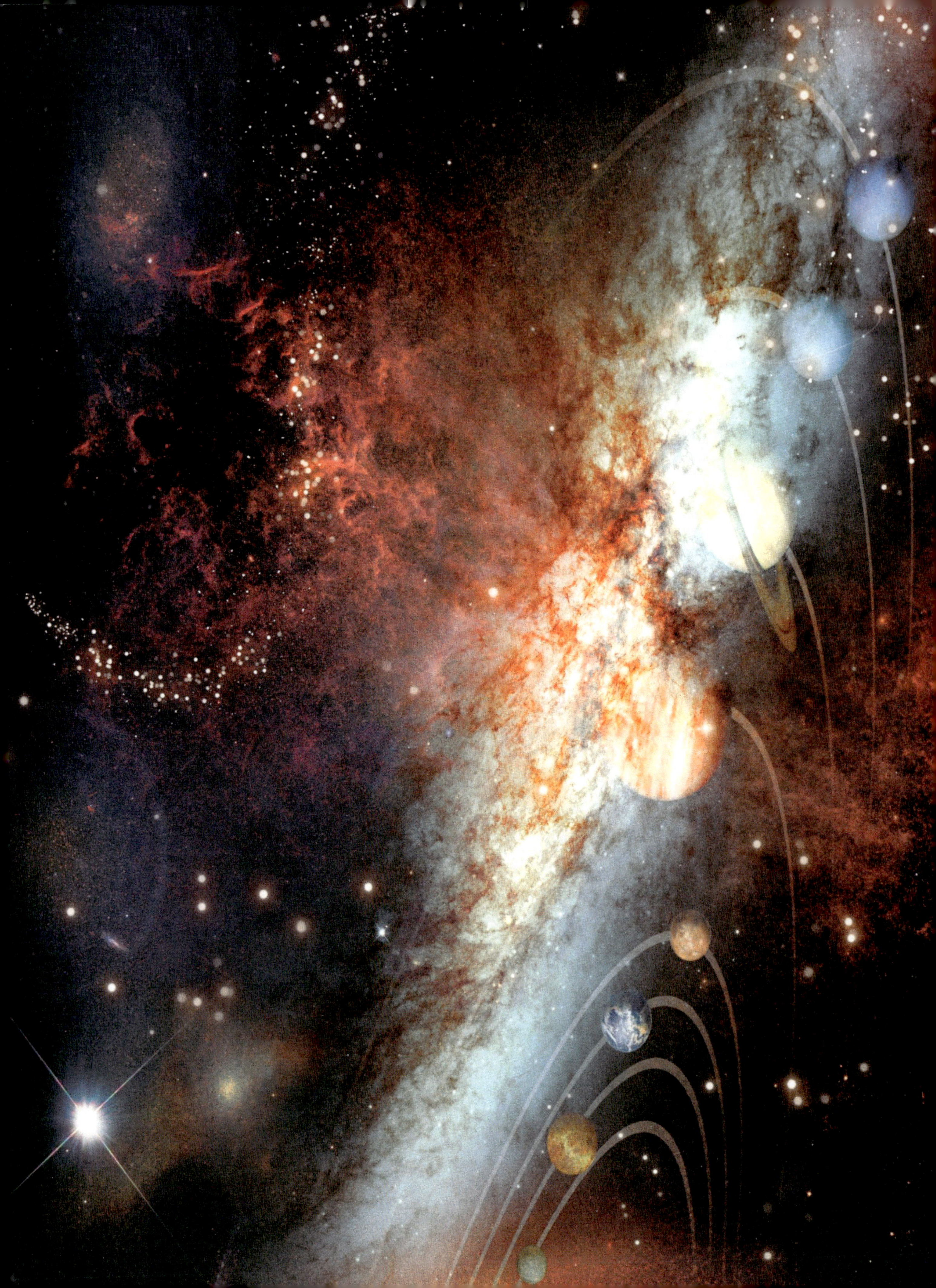

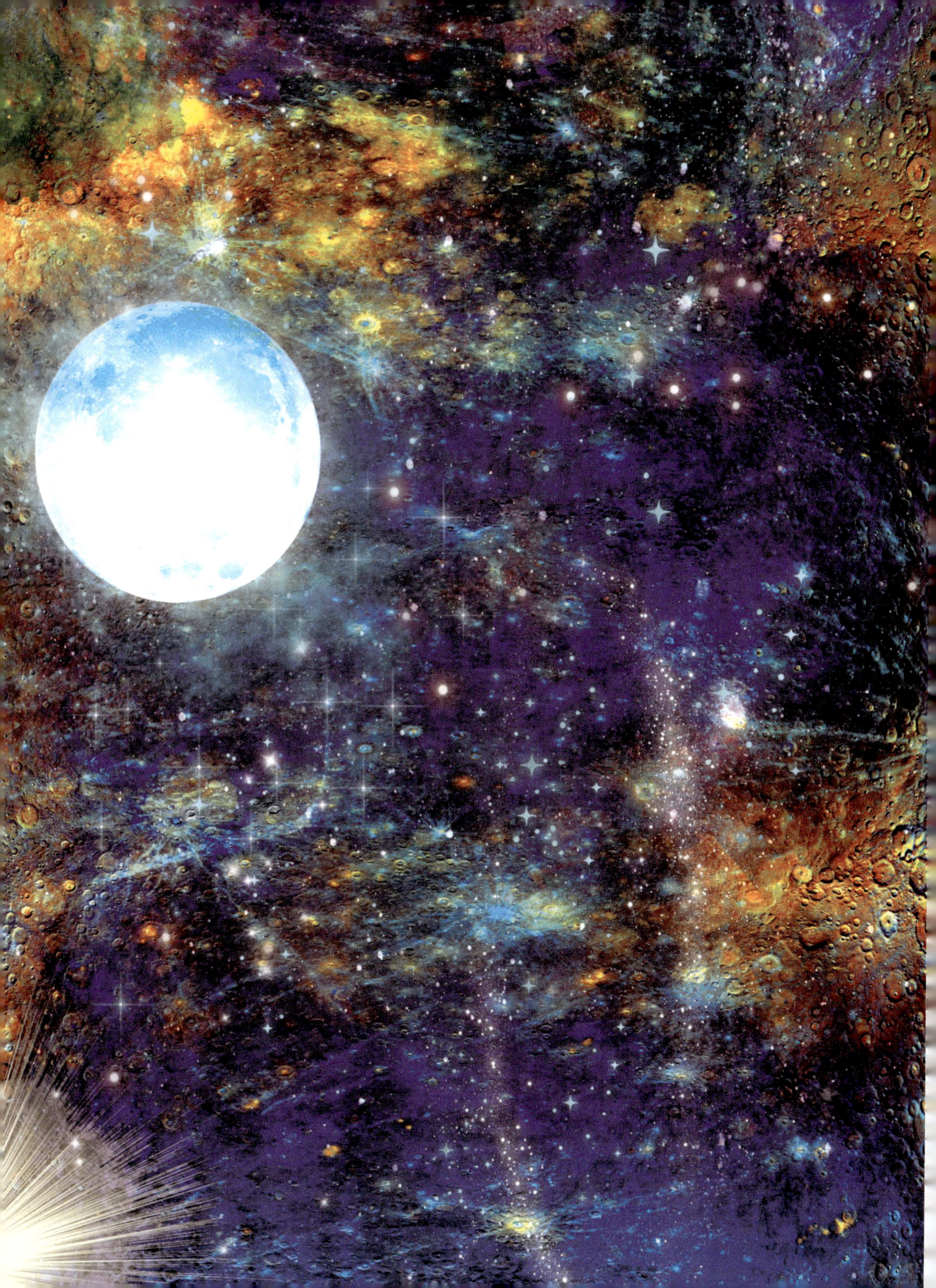

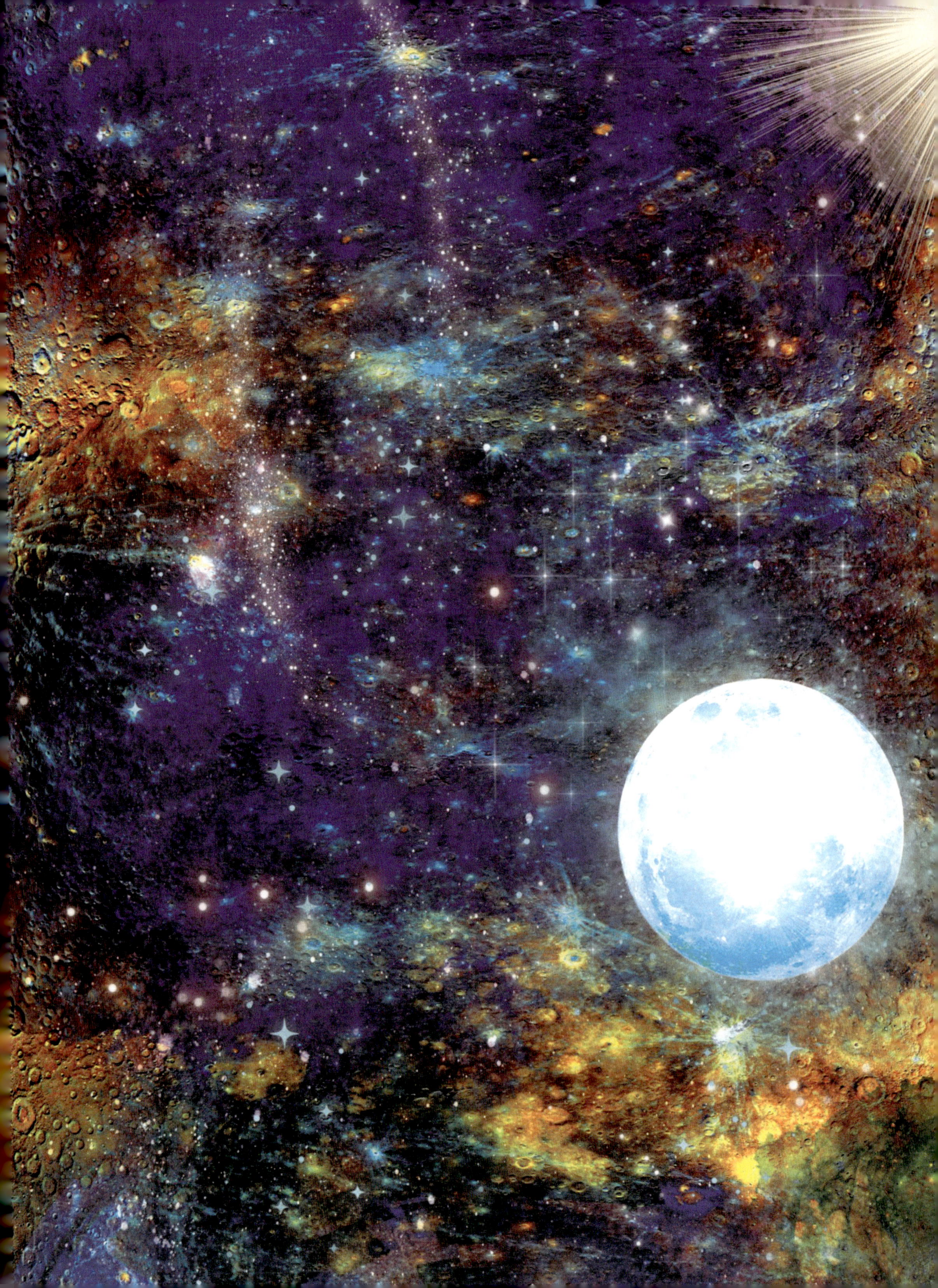

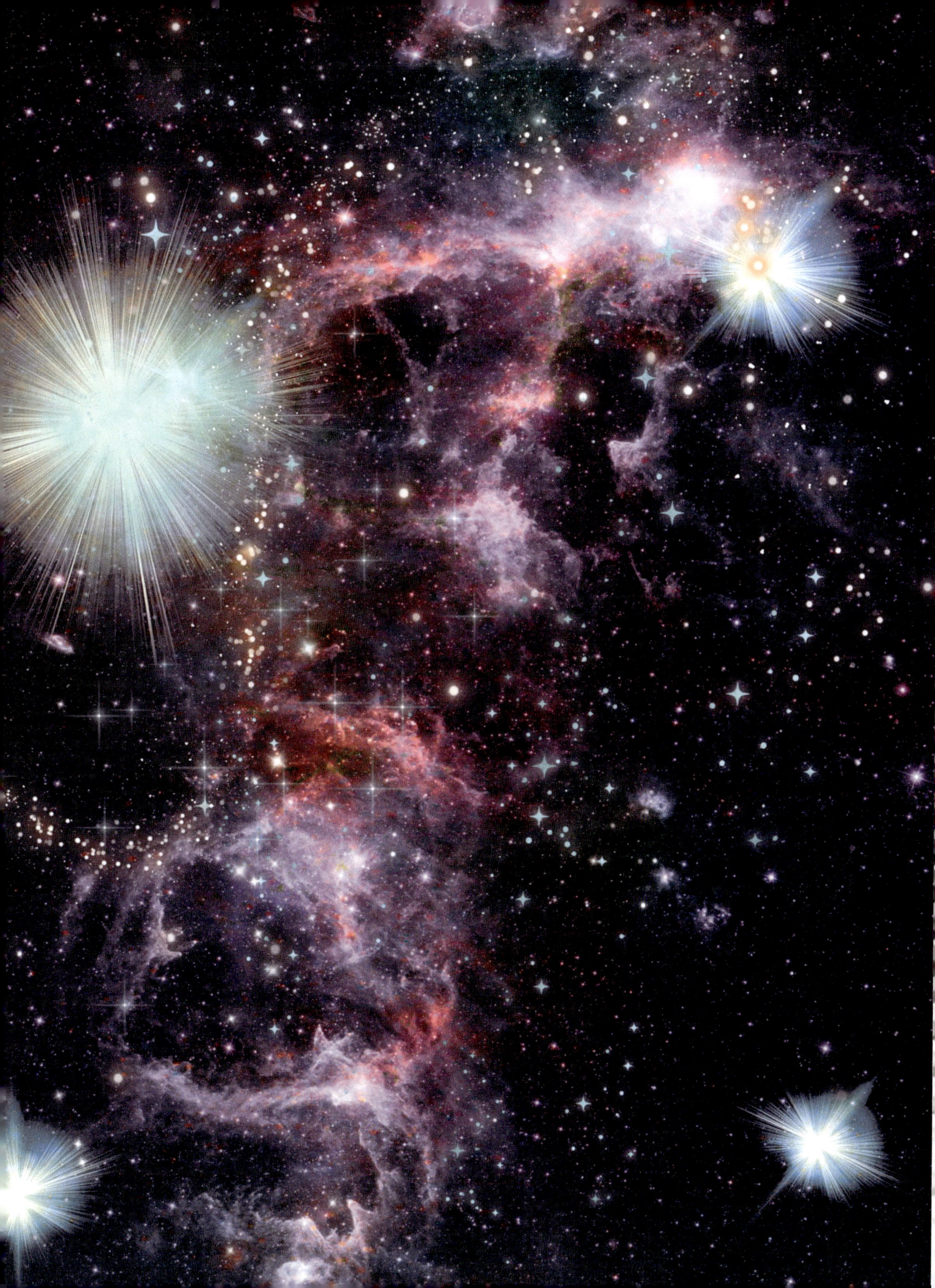

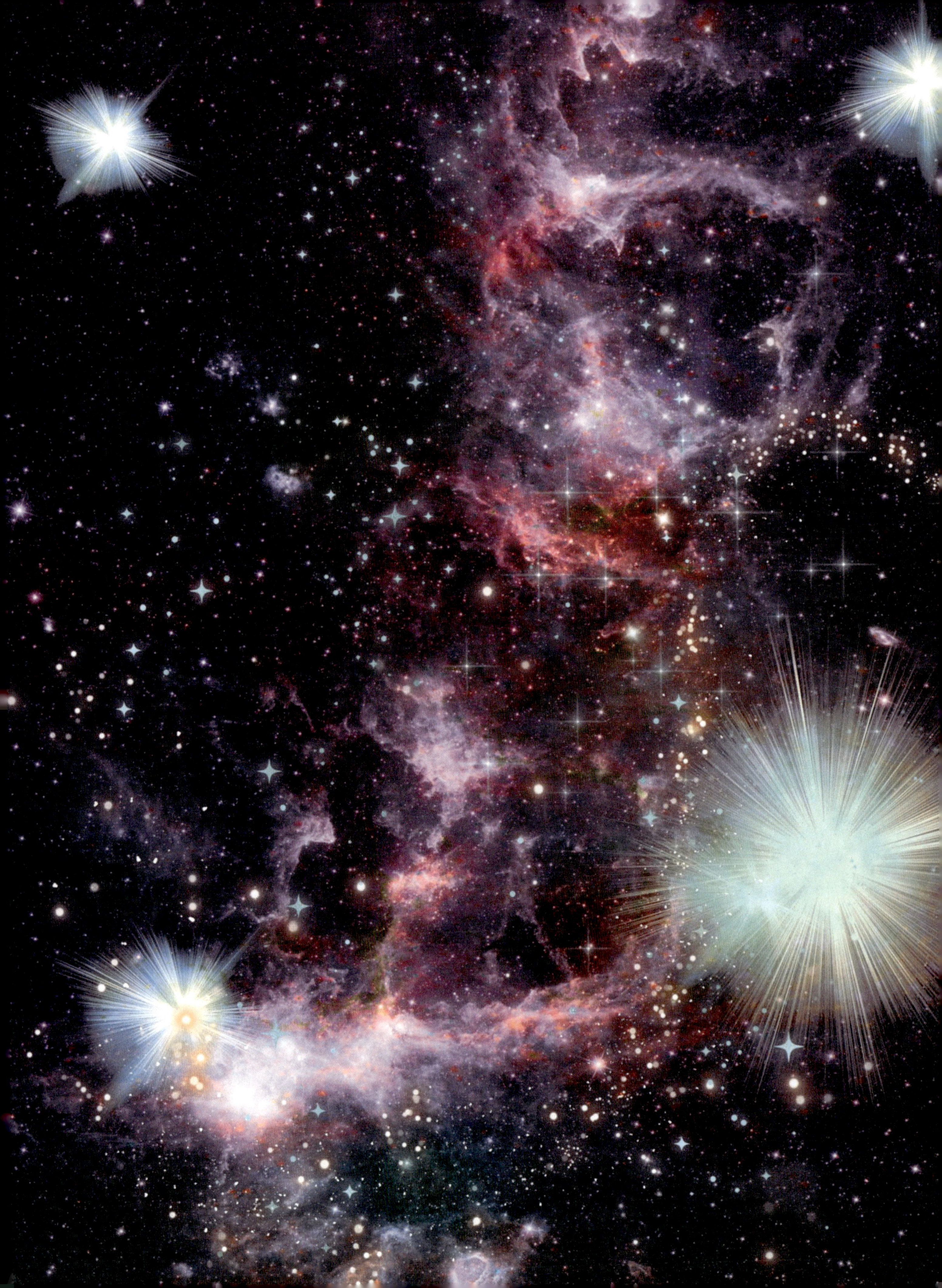

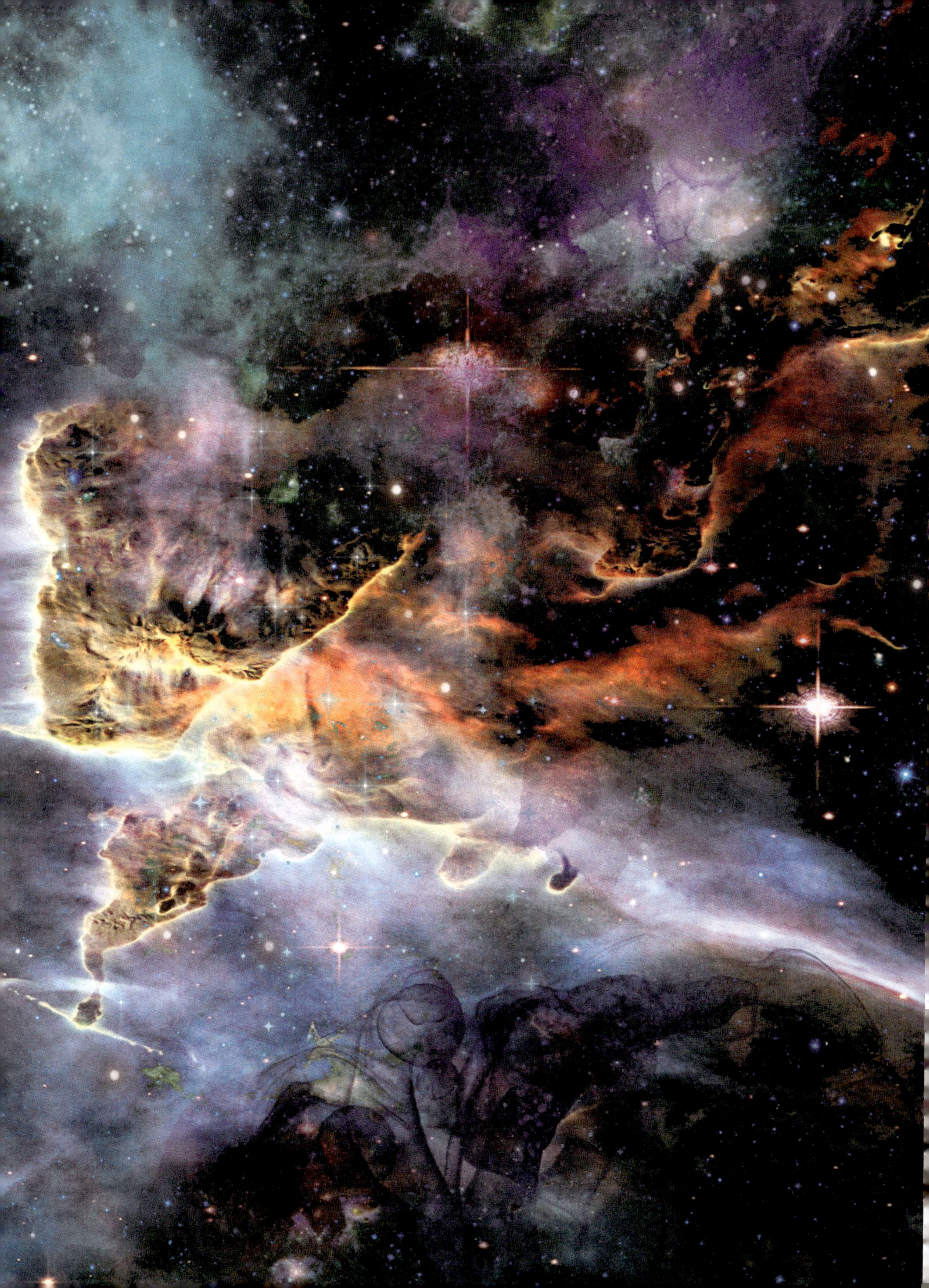

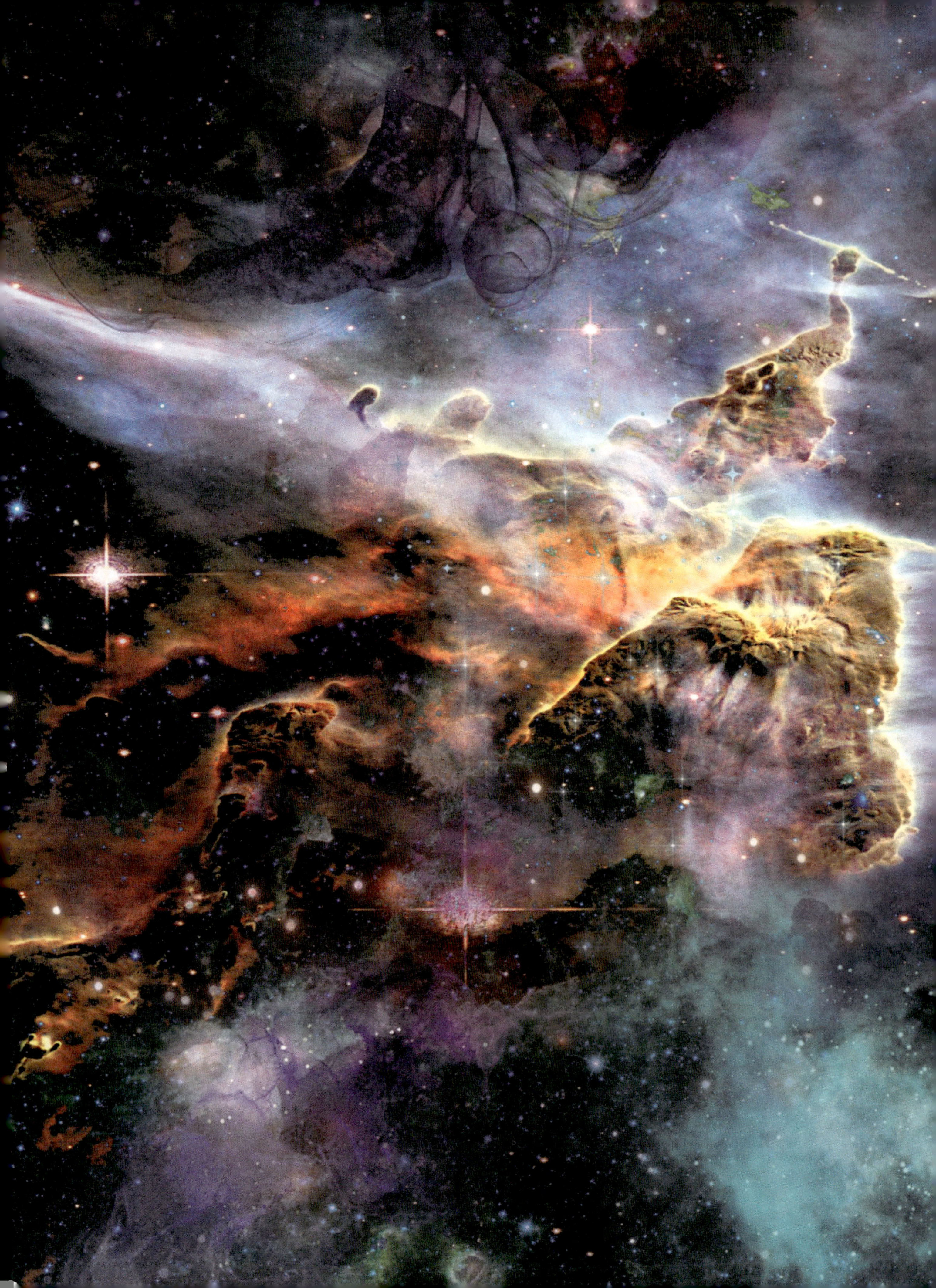

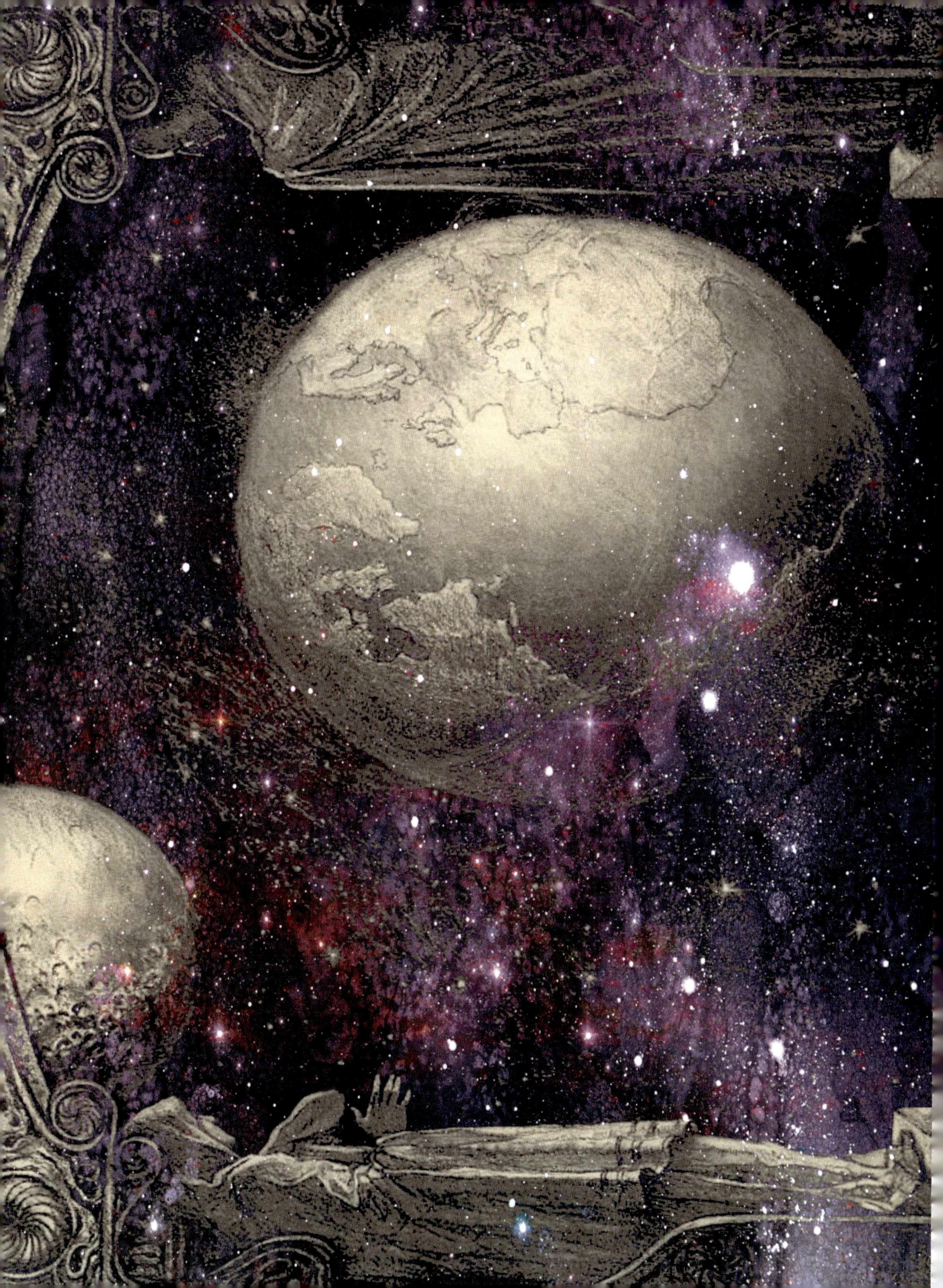

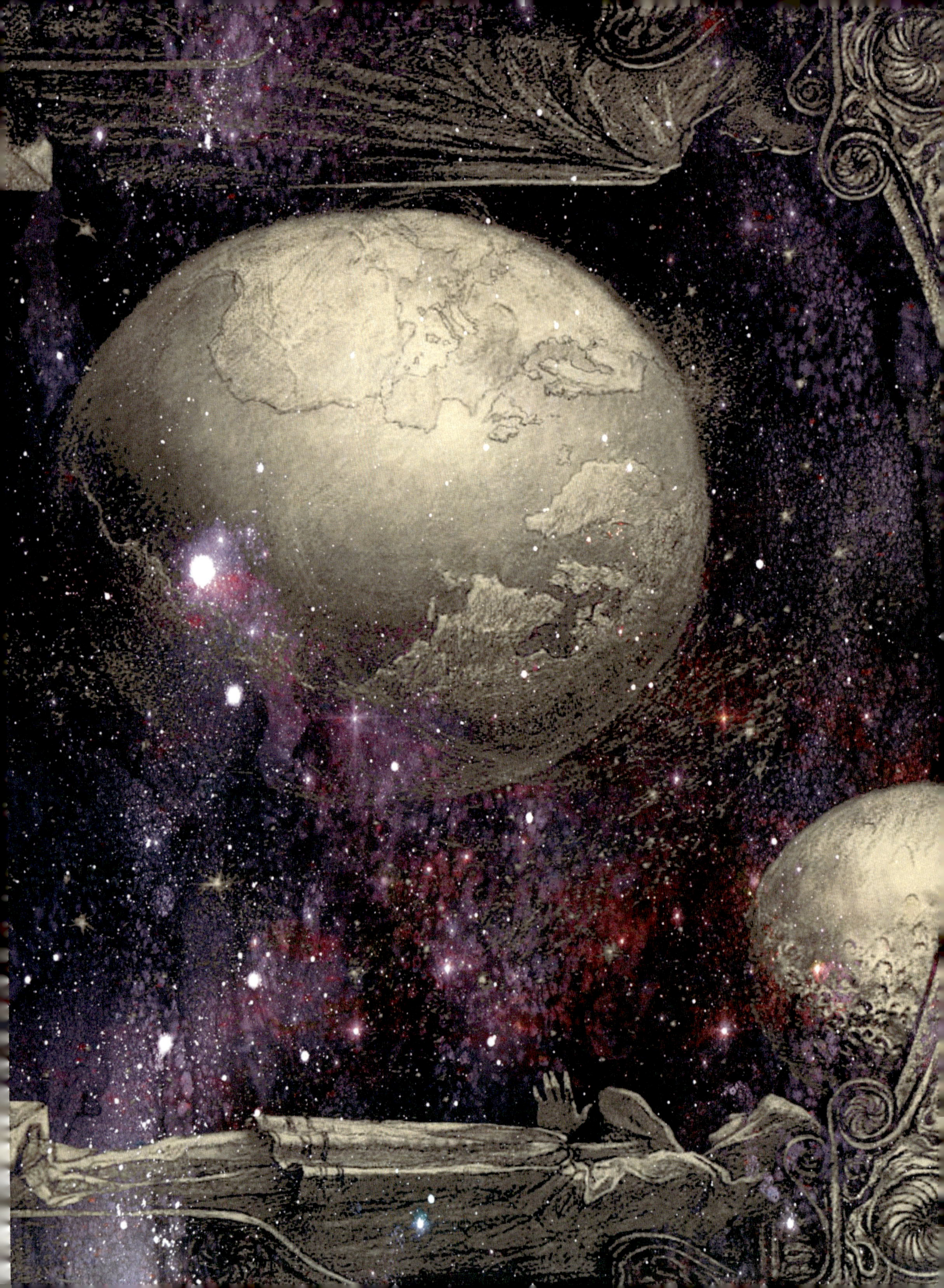

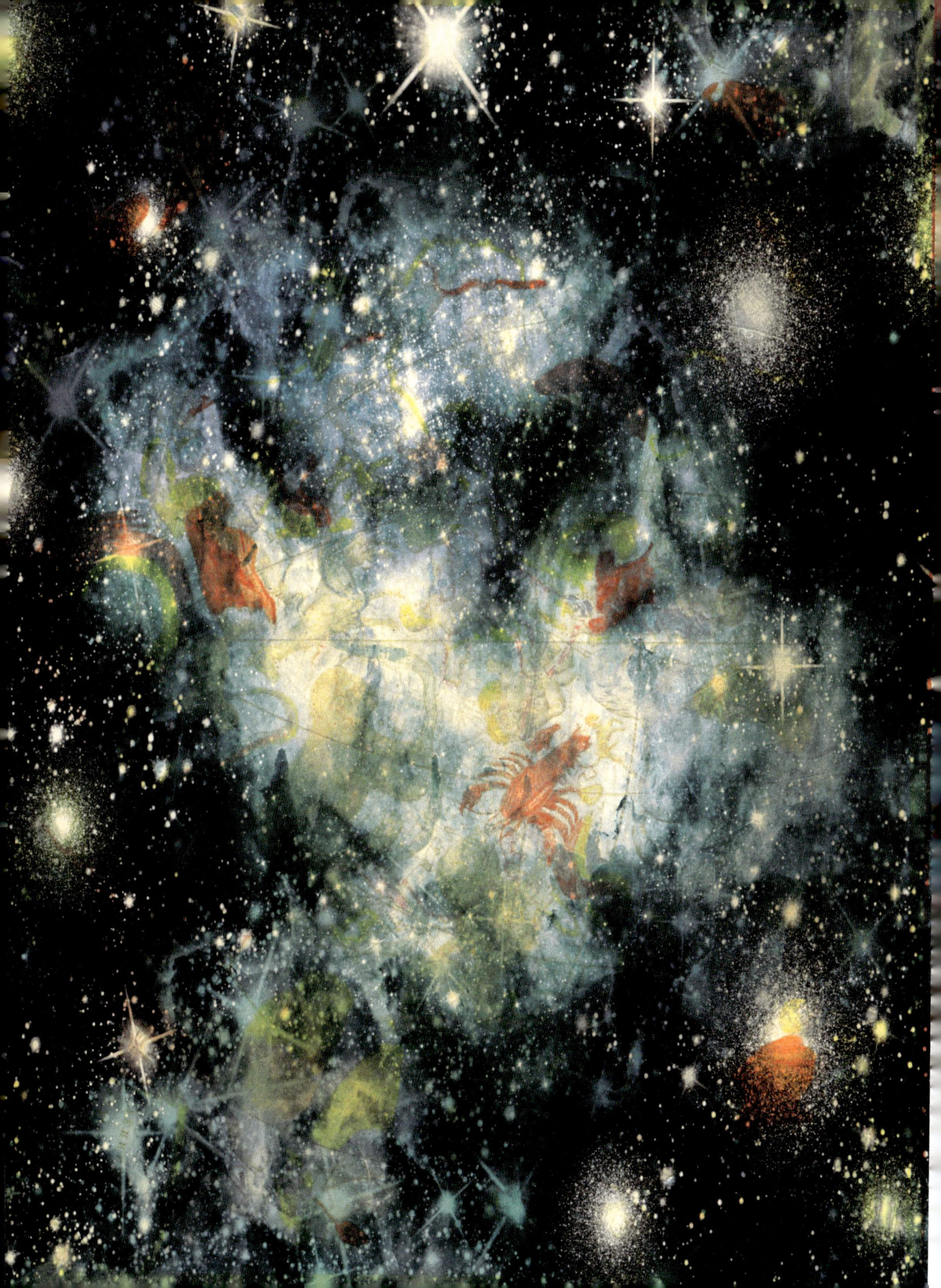

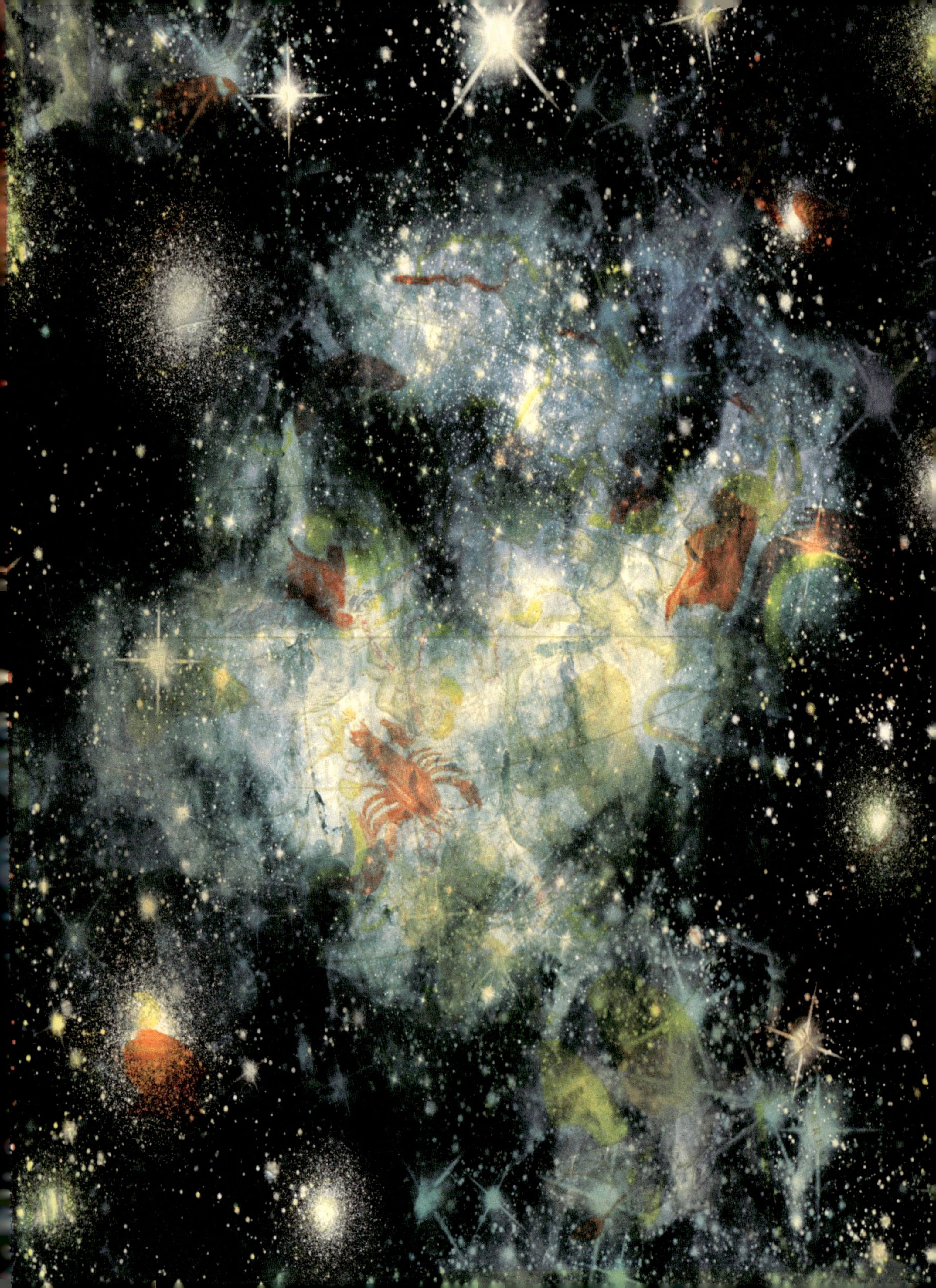

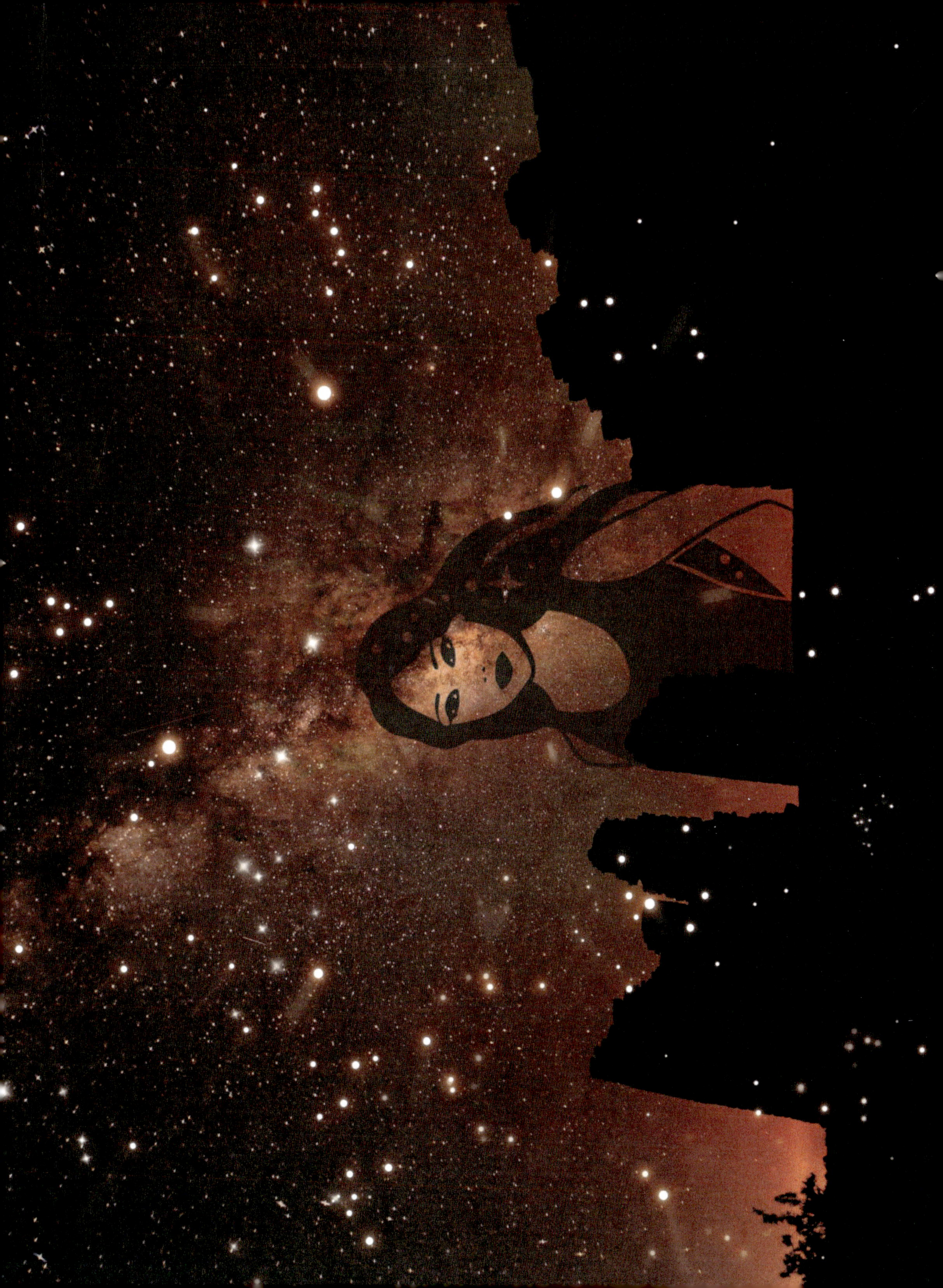

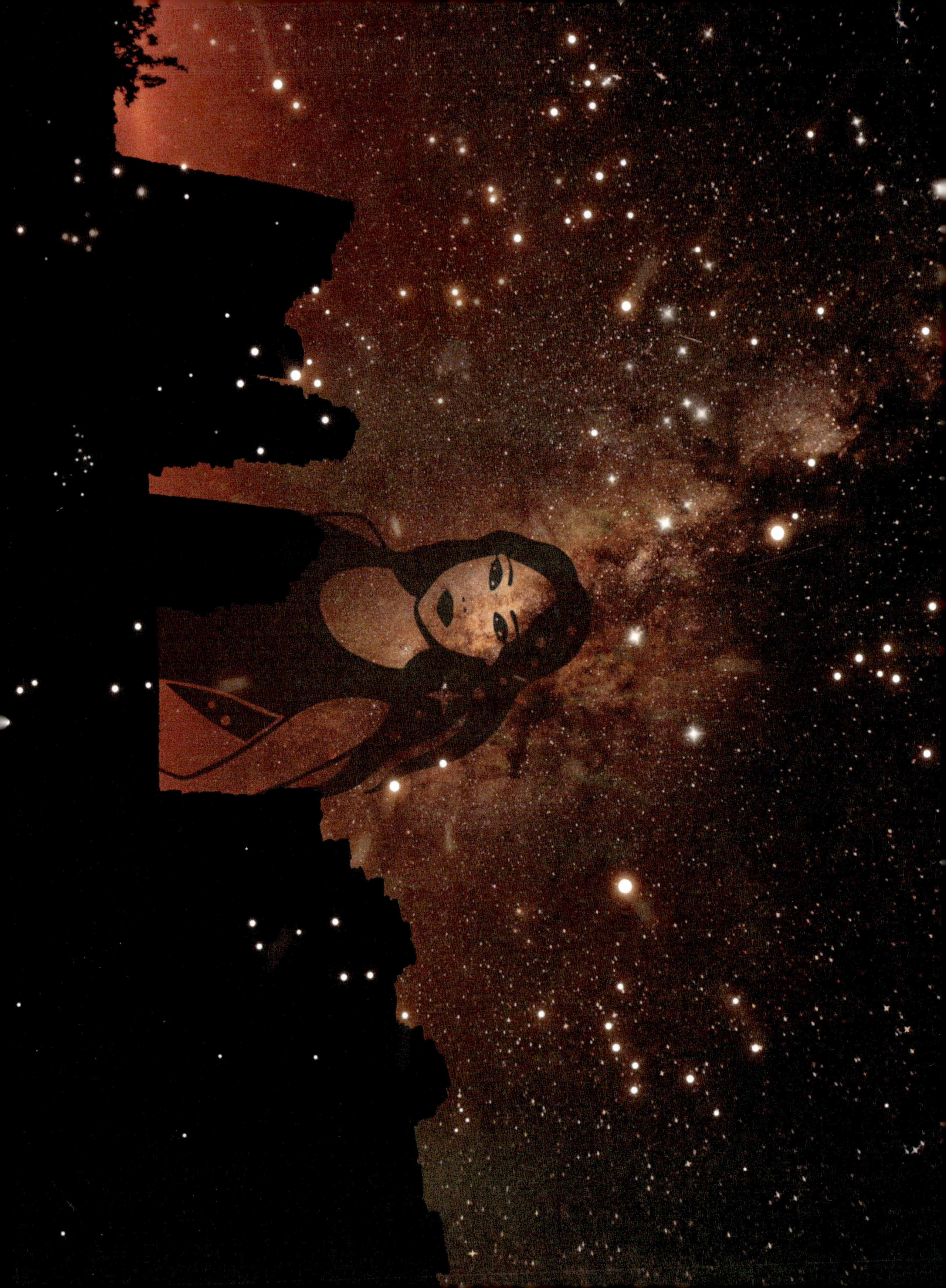

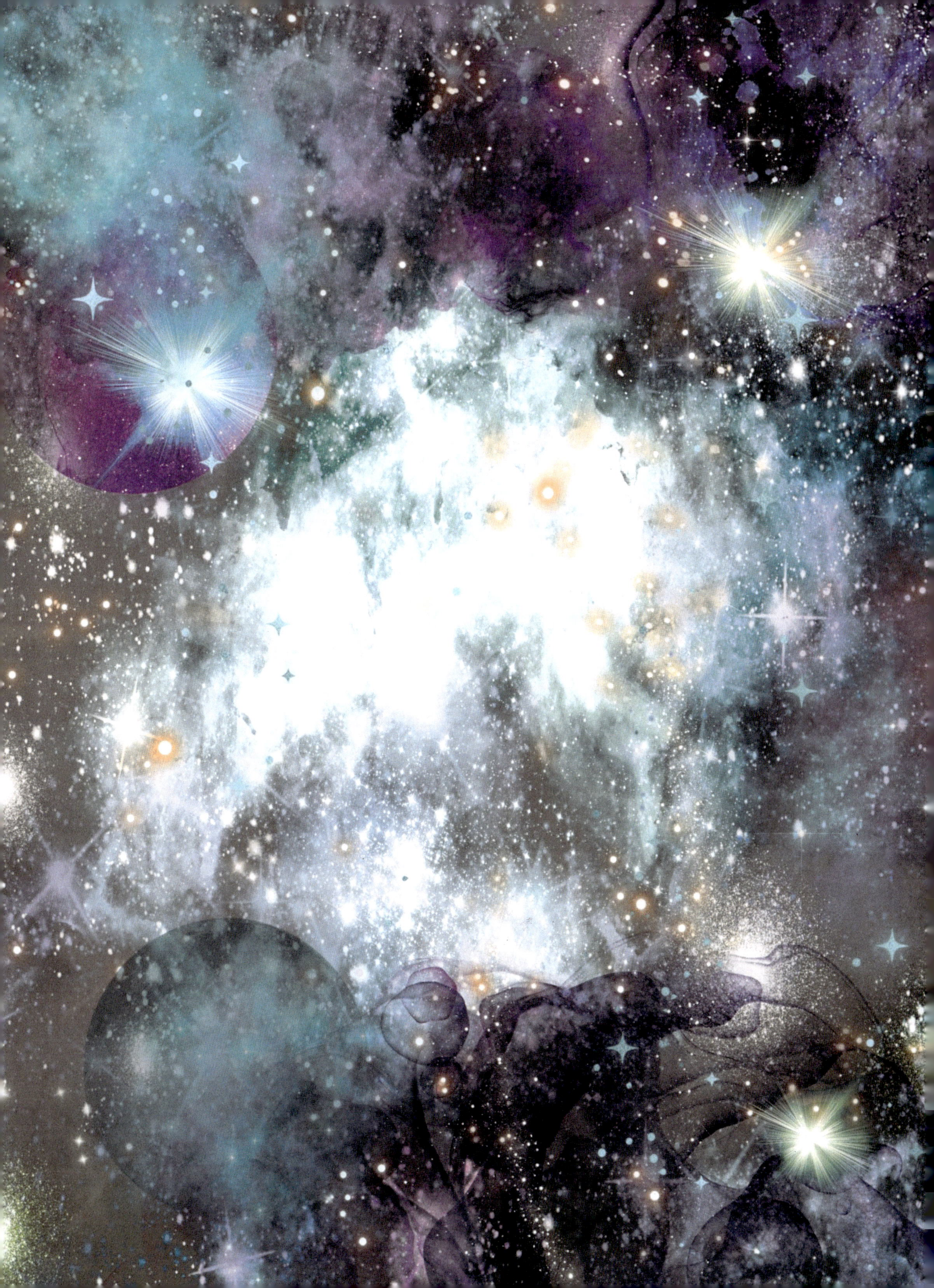

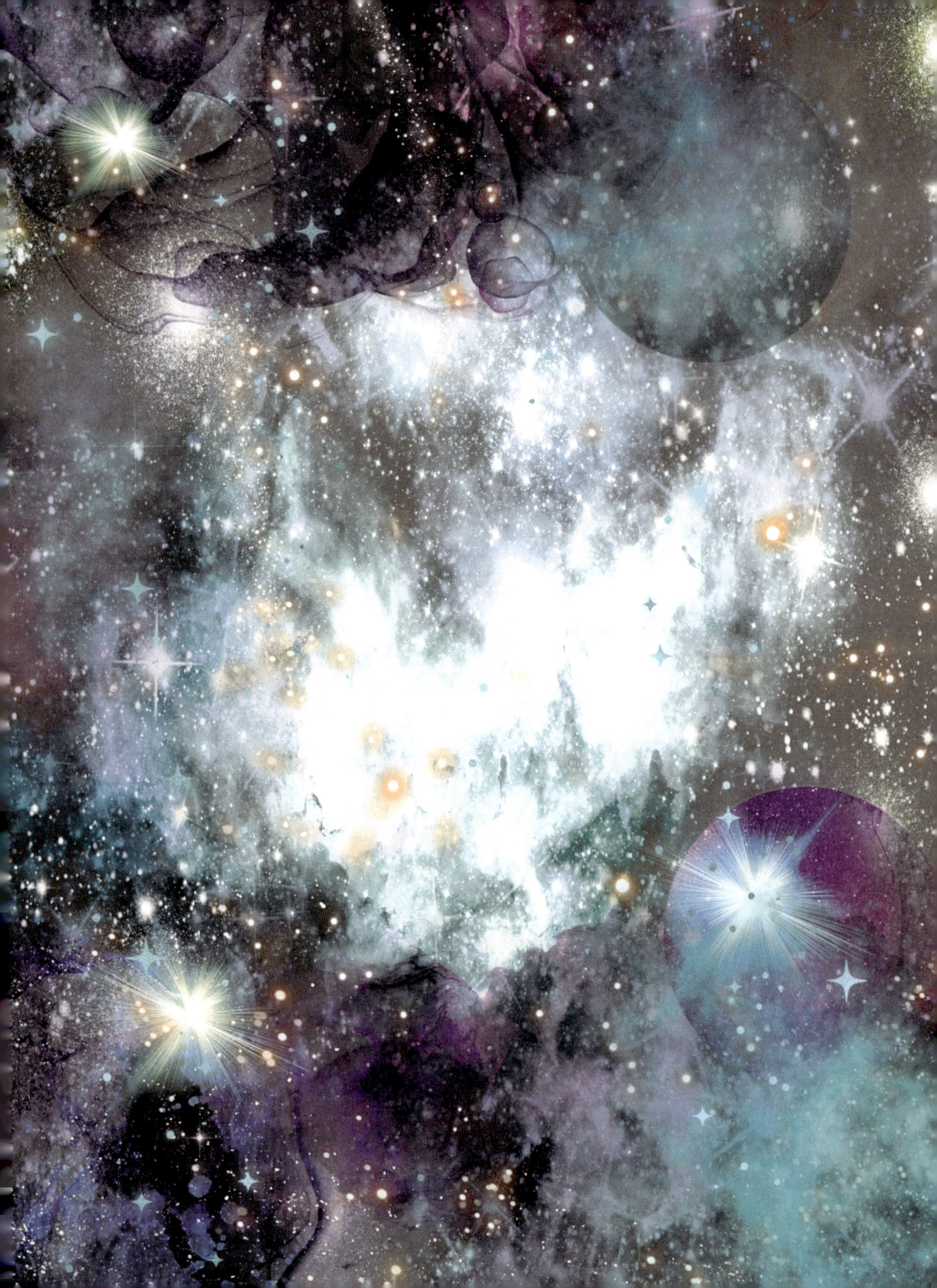

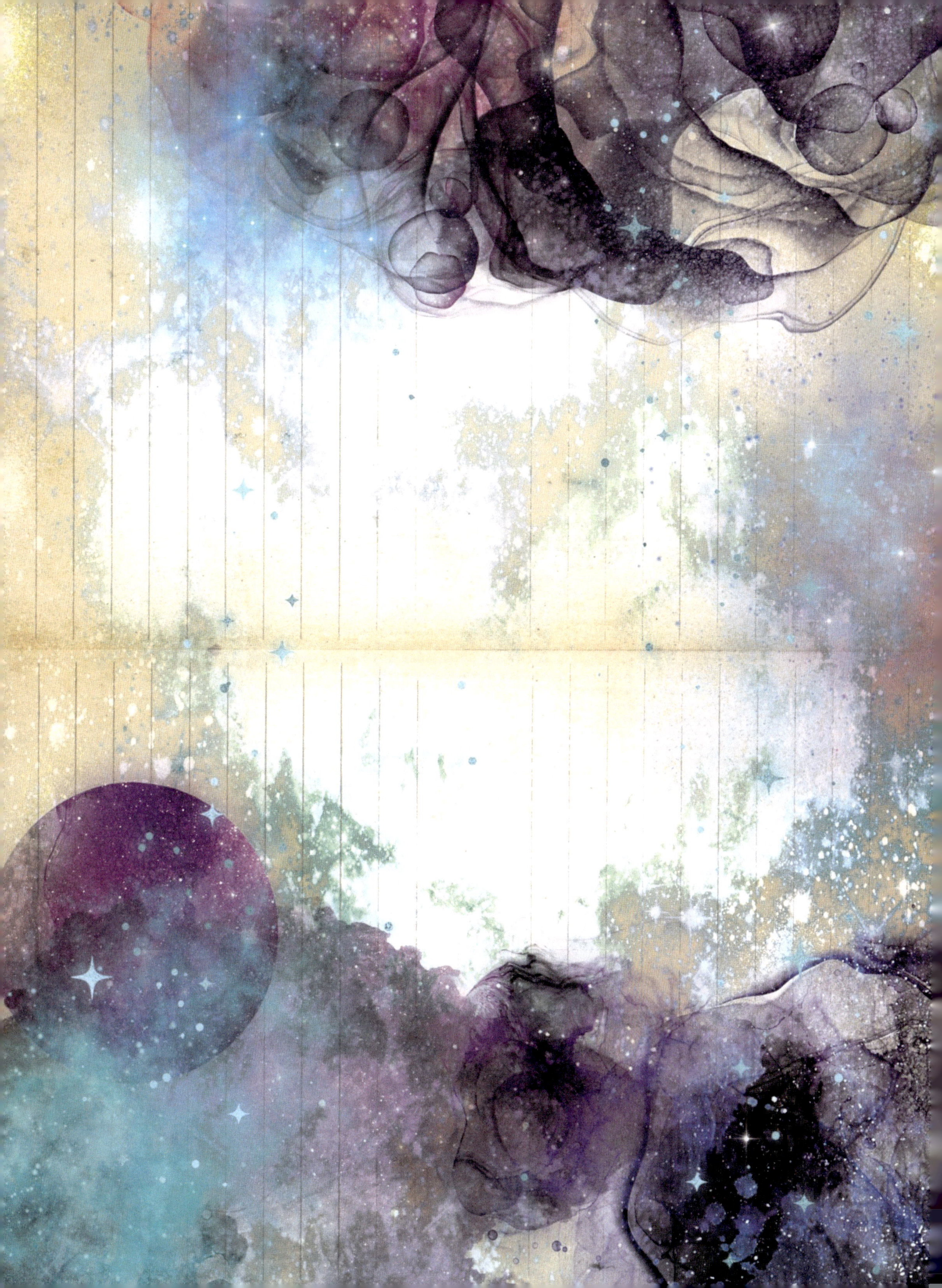

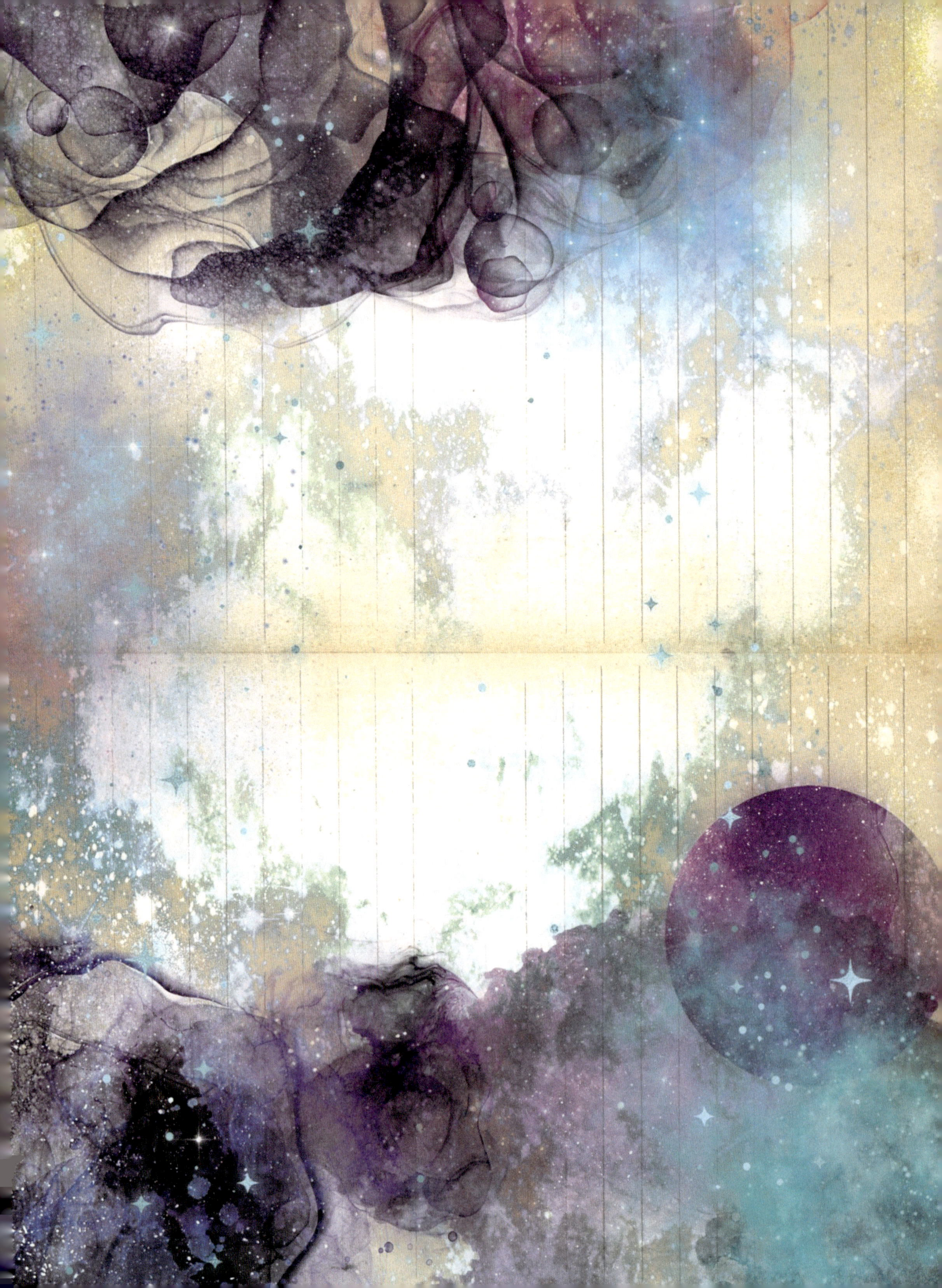

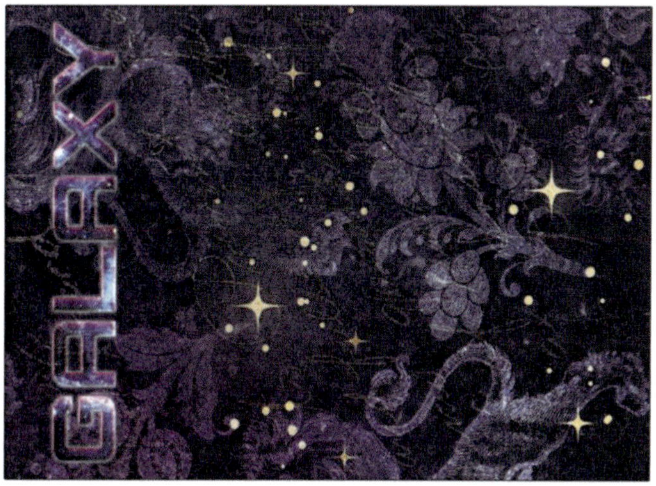
GALAXY
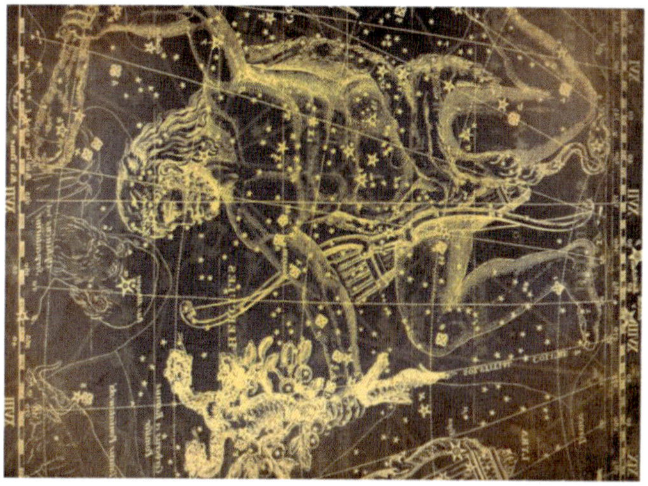
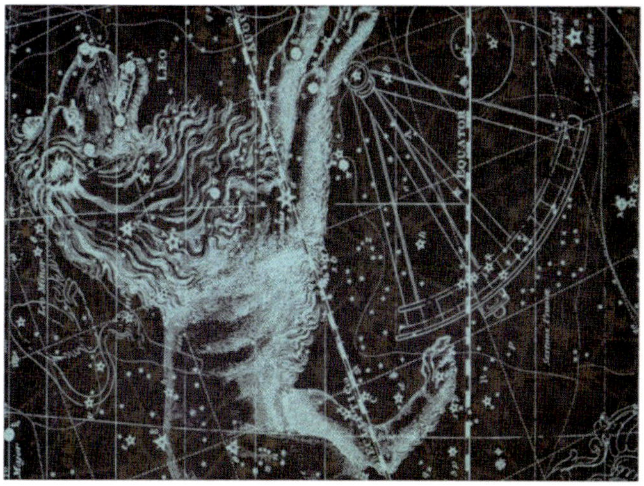
LEO
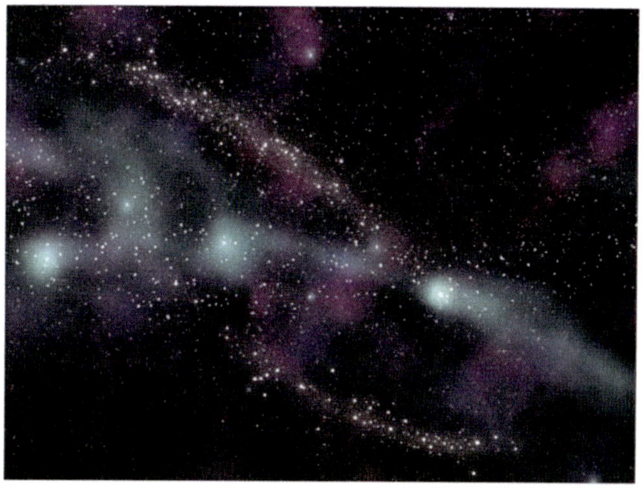
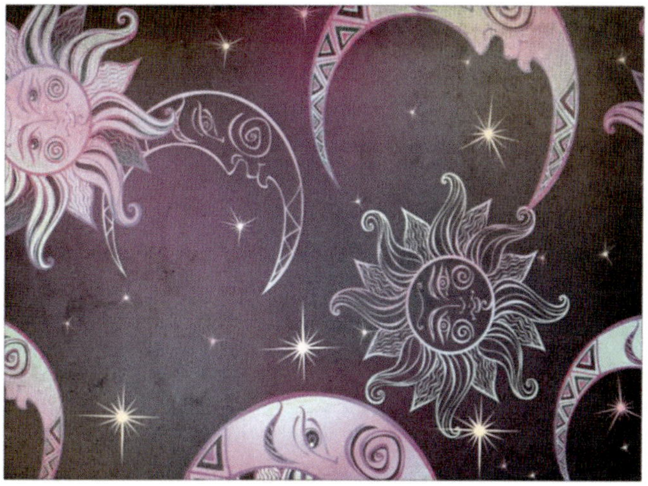
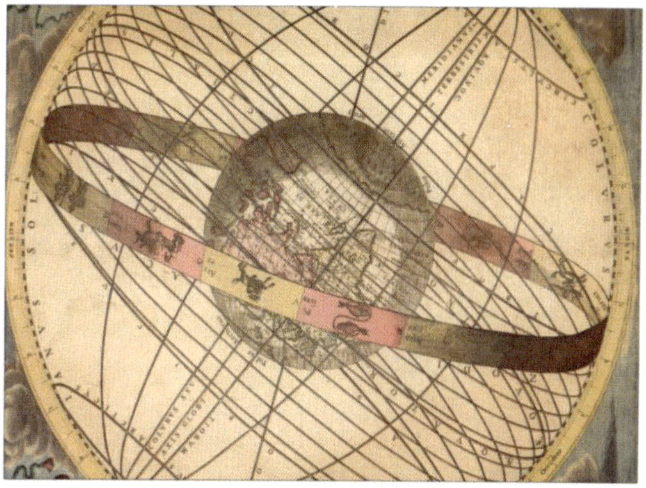
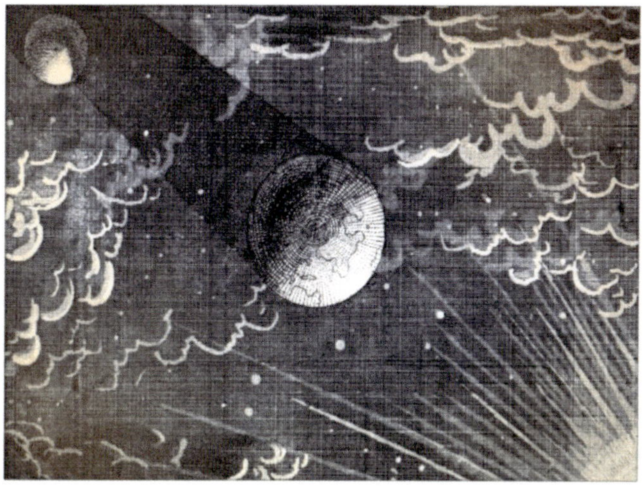
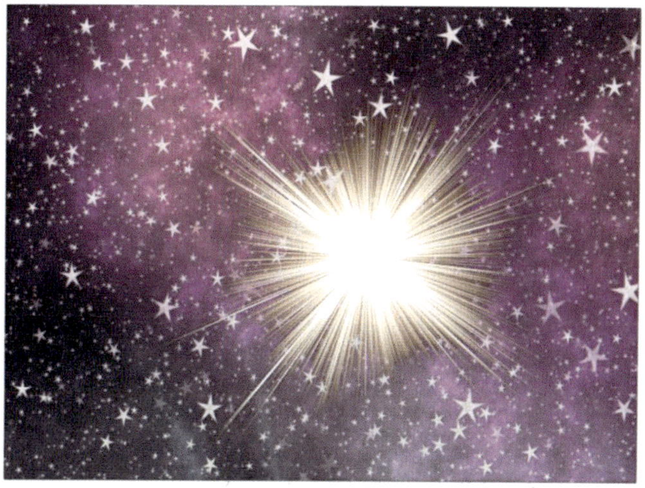

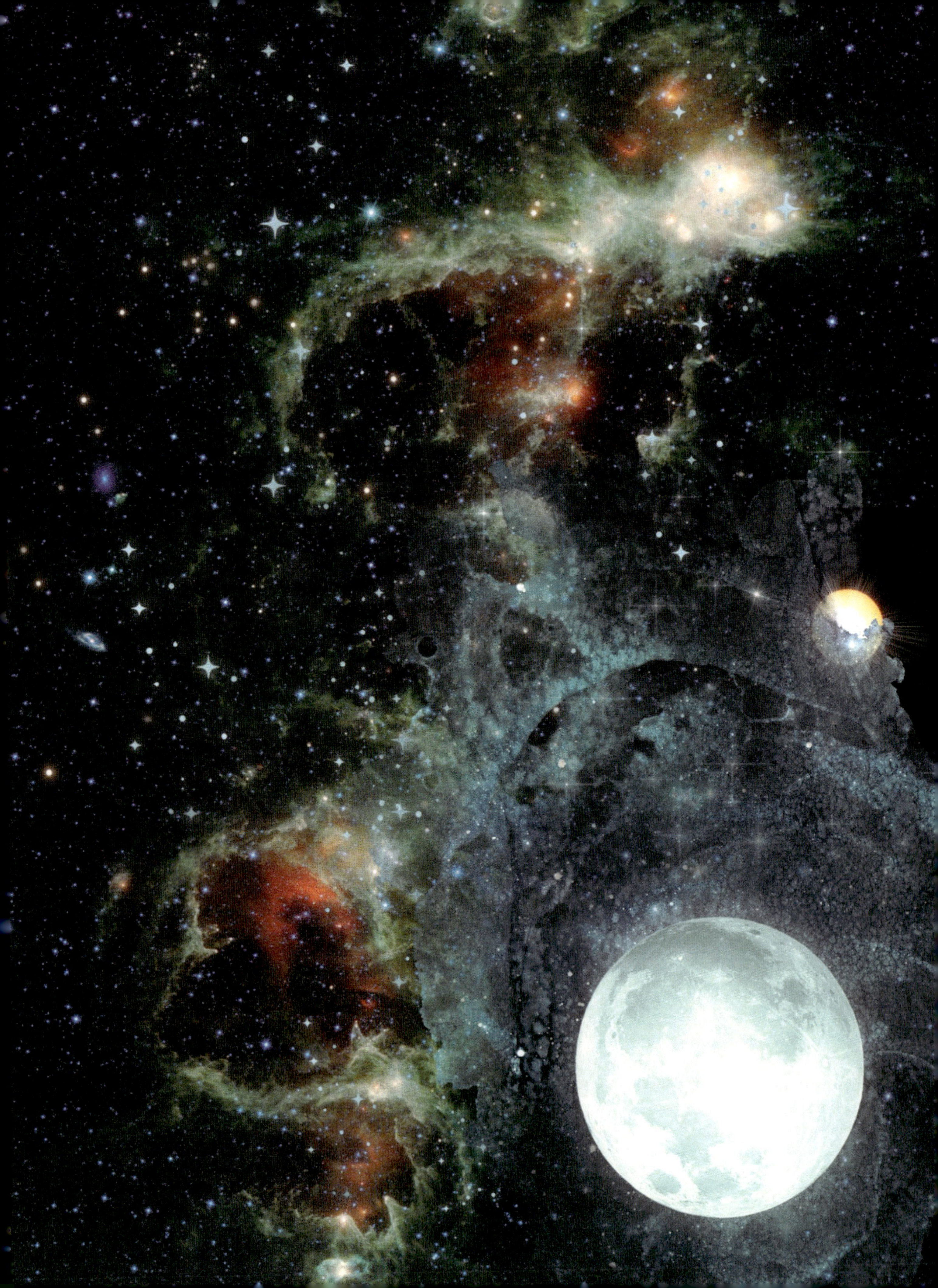

GALAXY

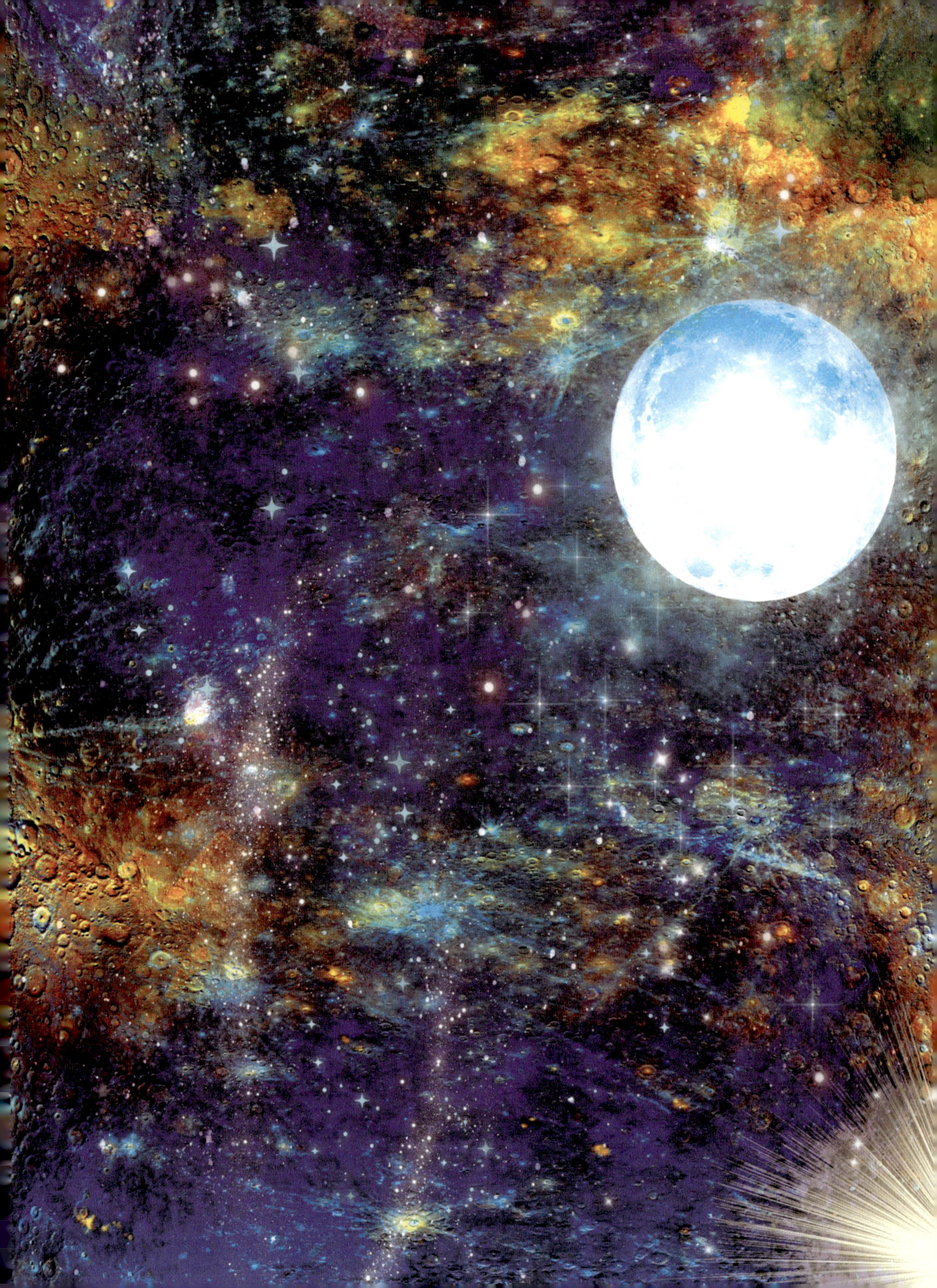

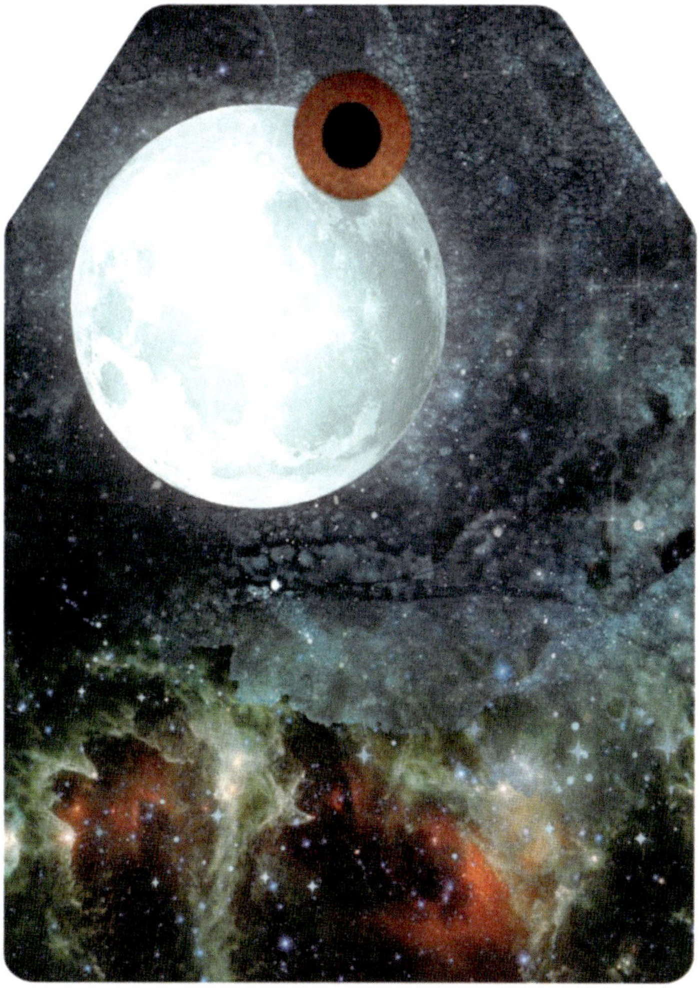

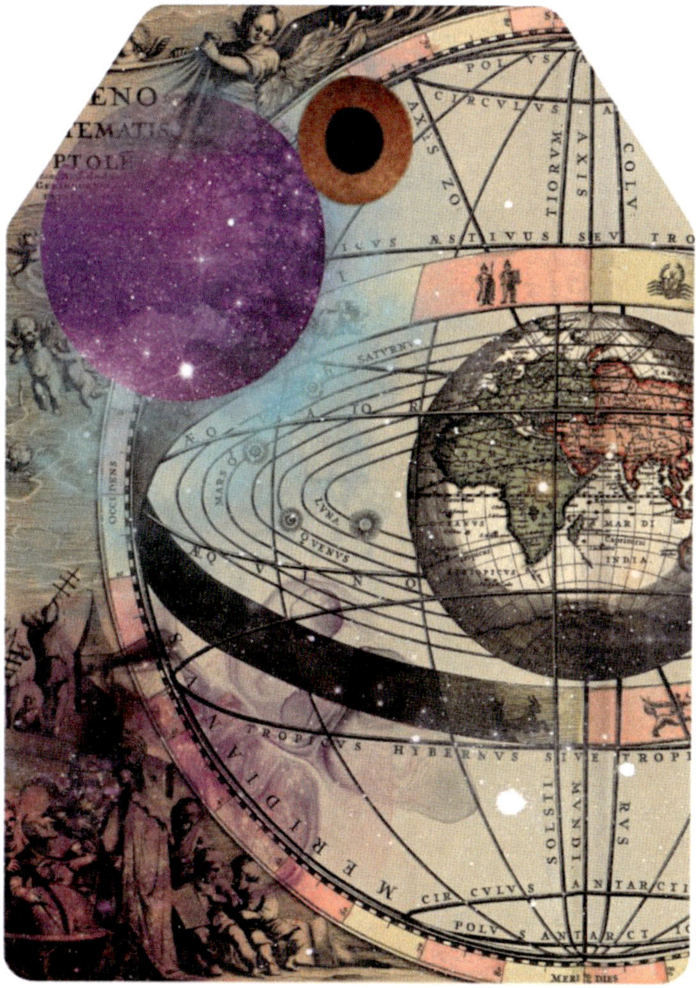
TROPICVS HYBERNVS SIVE
MERIDIANVS
CIRCVLVS
LVNA
INDIA

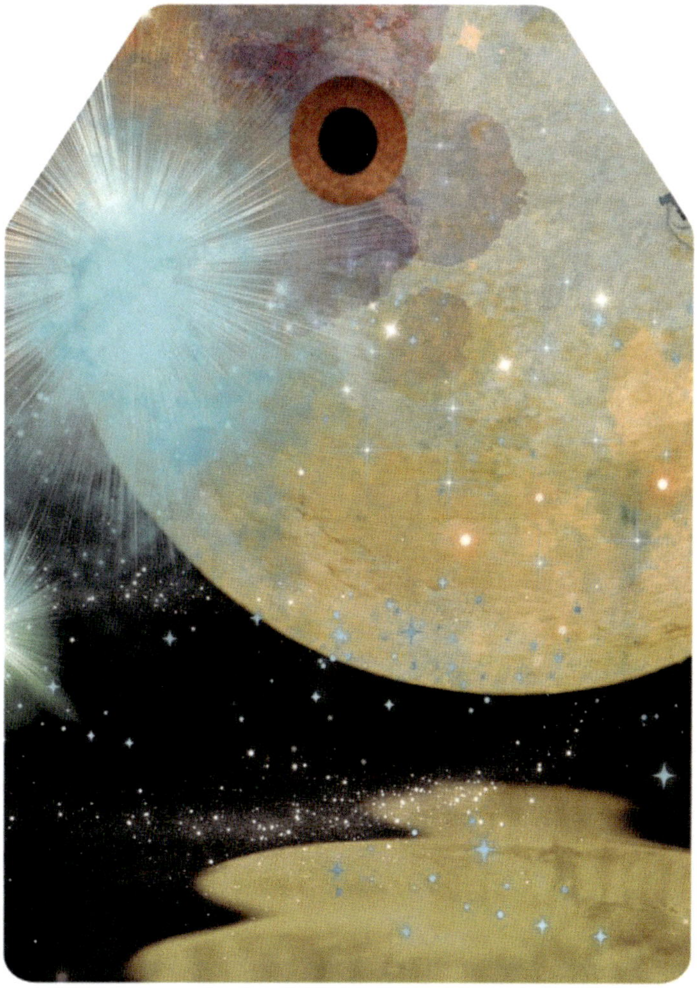

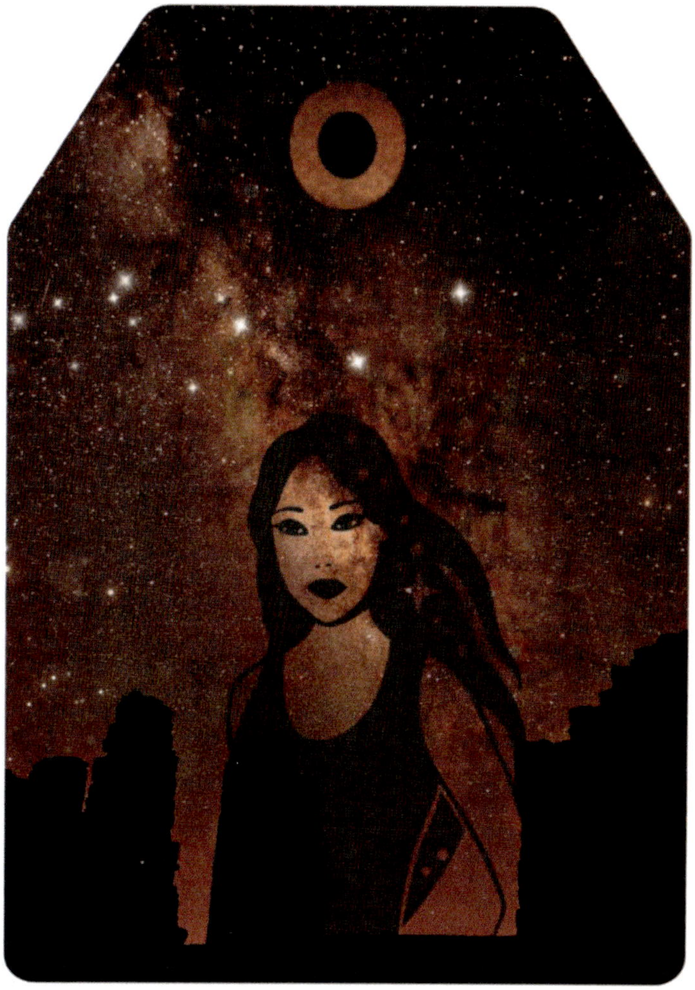

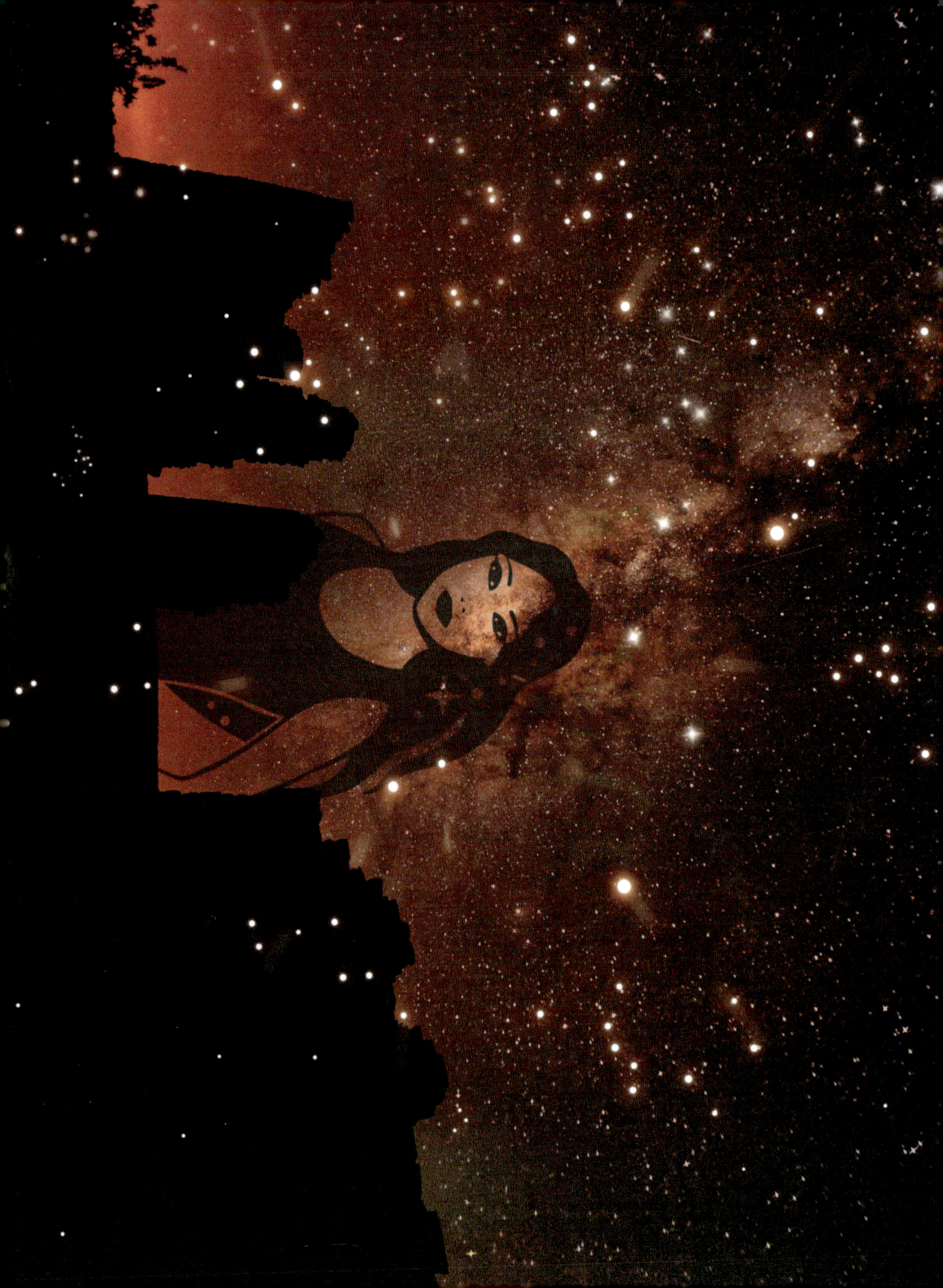

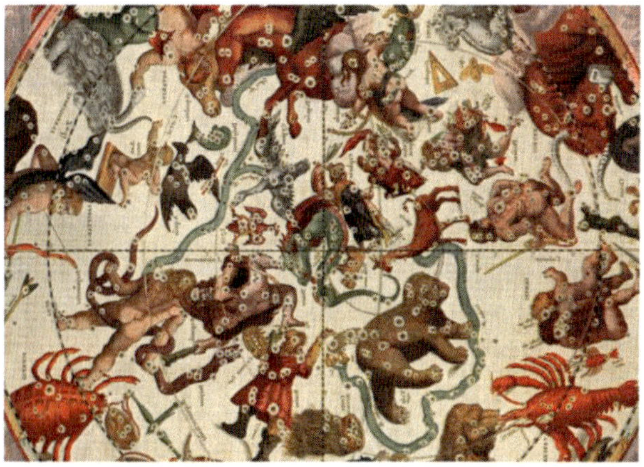
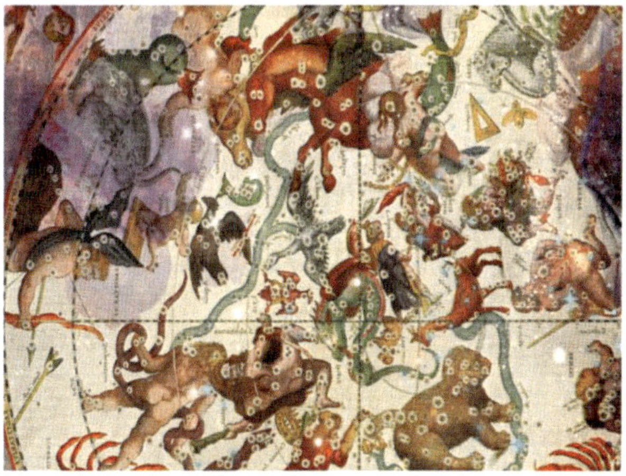
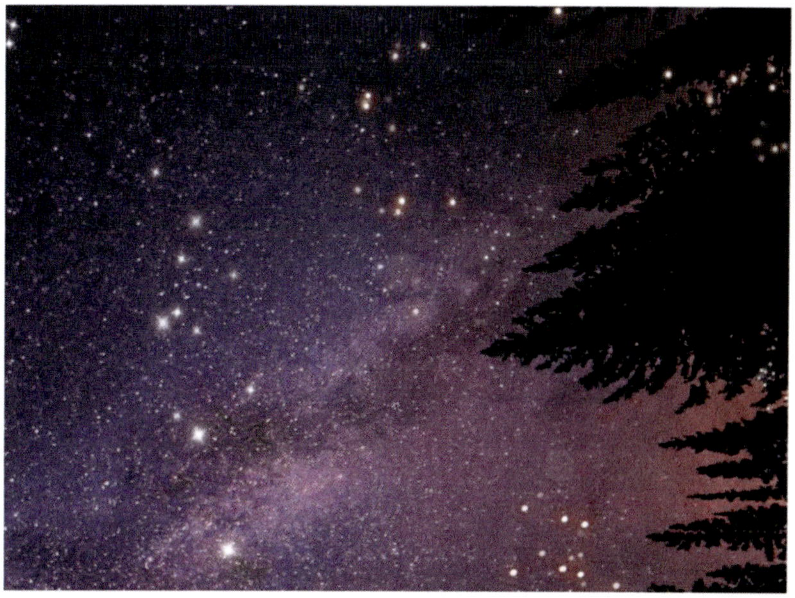
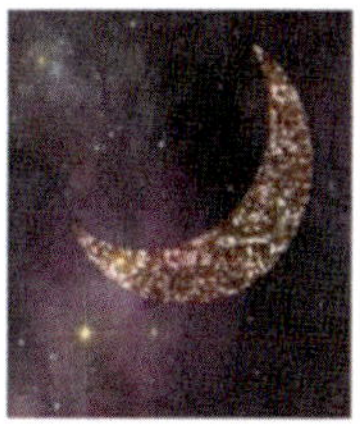
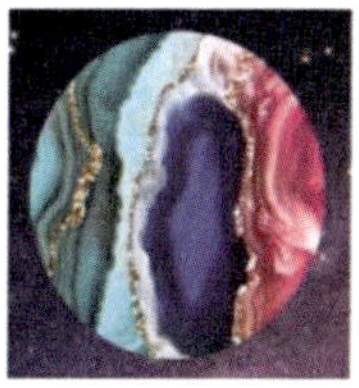
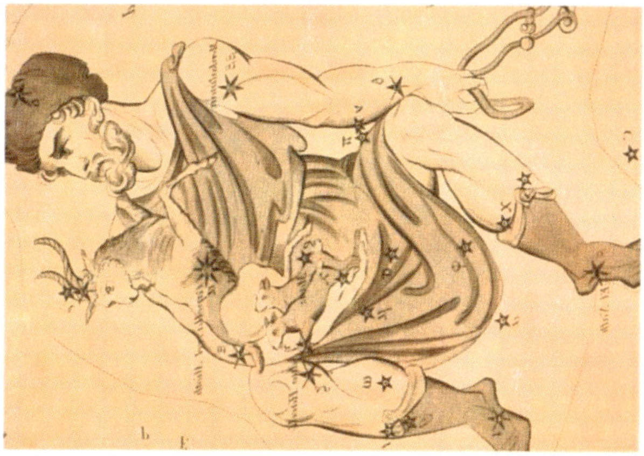
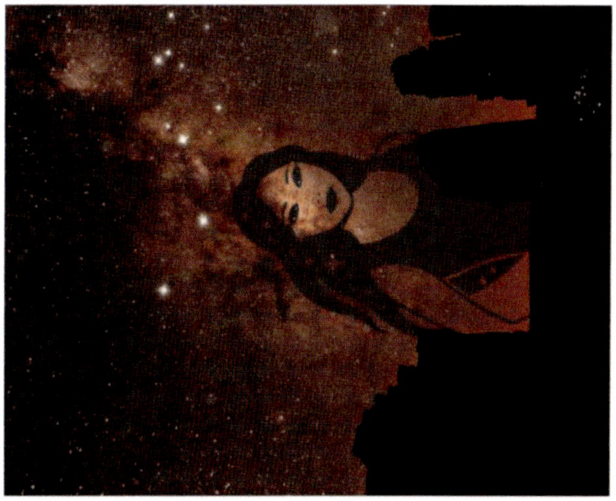
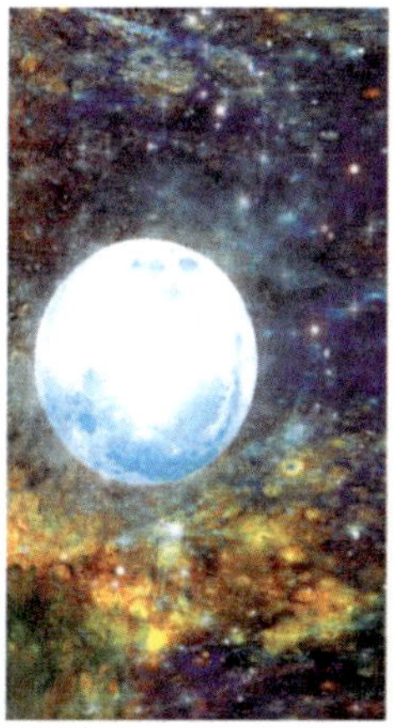
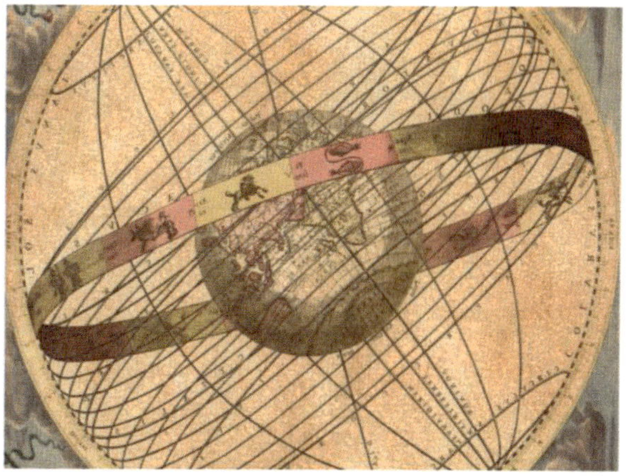
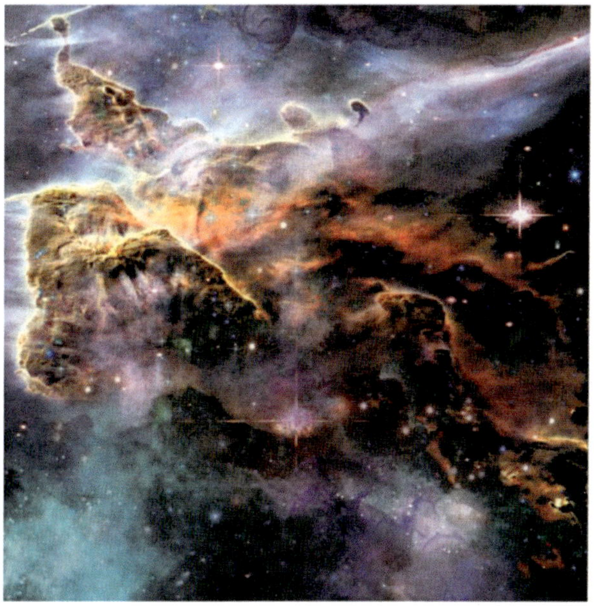
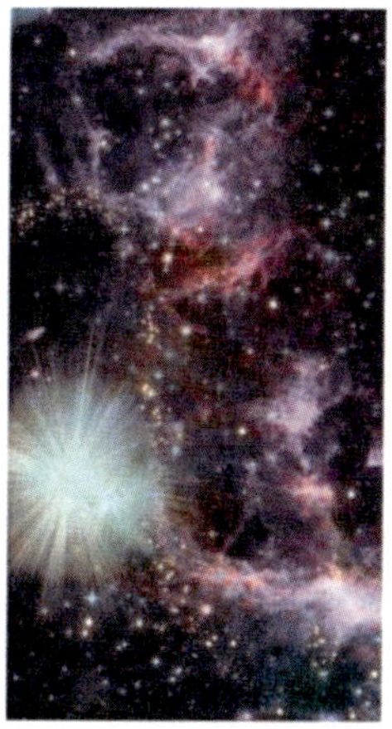
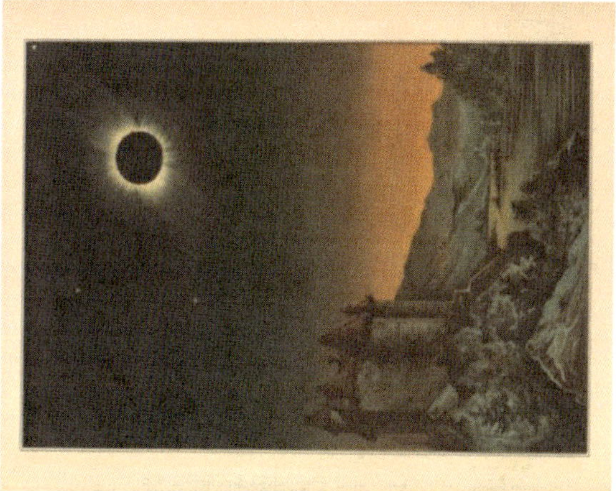

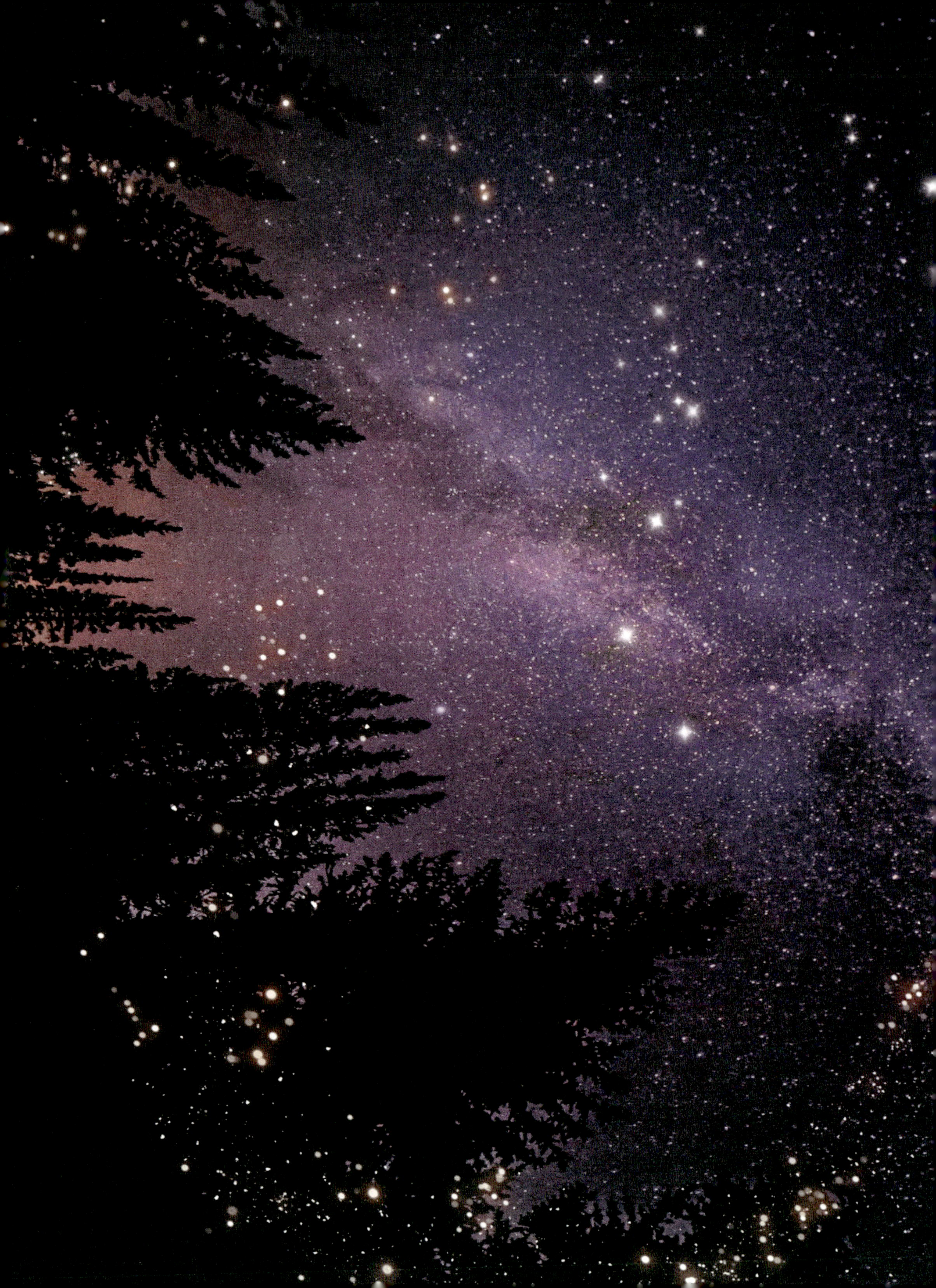

Post Card

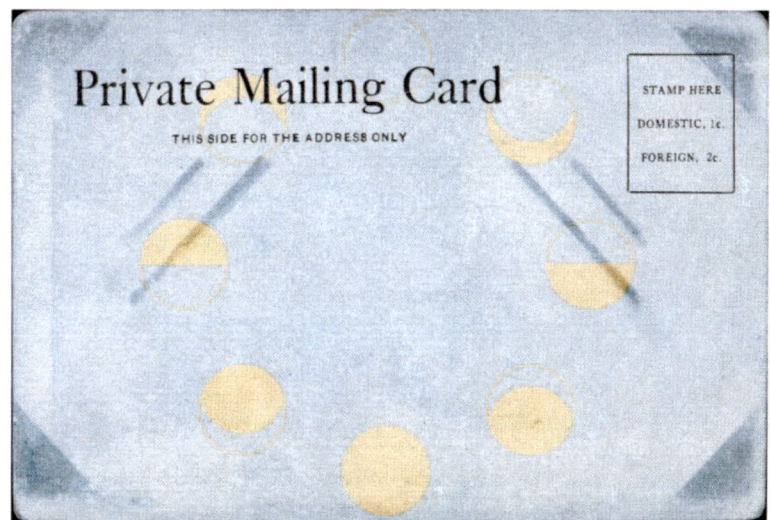

Private Mailing Card
THIS SIDE FOR THE ADDRESS ONLY
STAMP HERE
DOMESTIC, 1c.
FOREIGN, 2c.

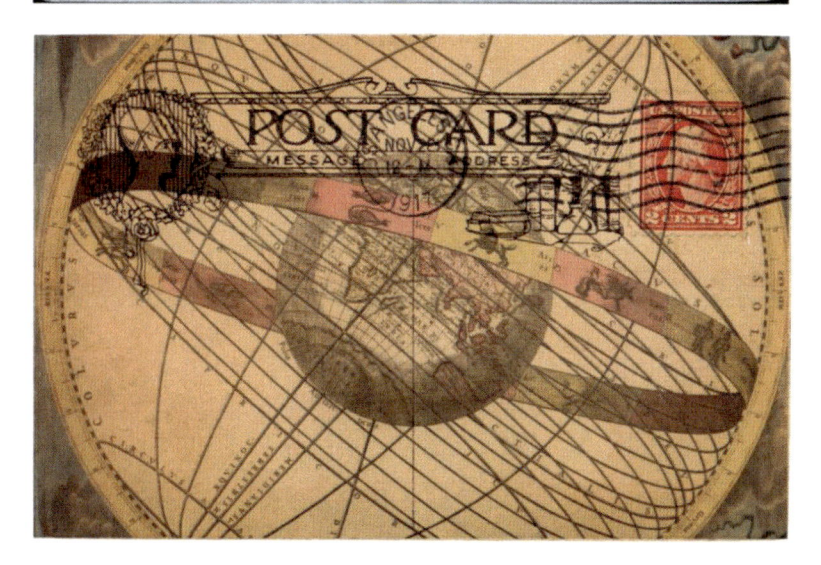

POST CARD

Carte Postale

POSTAL CARD

POST CARD

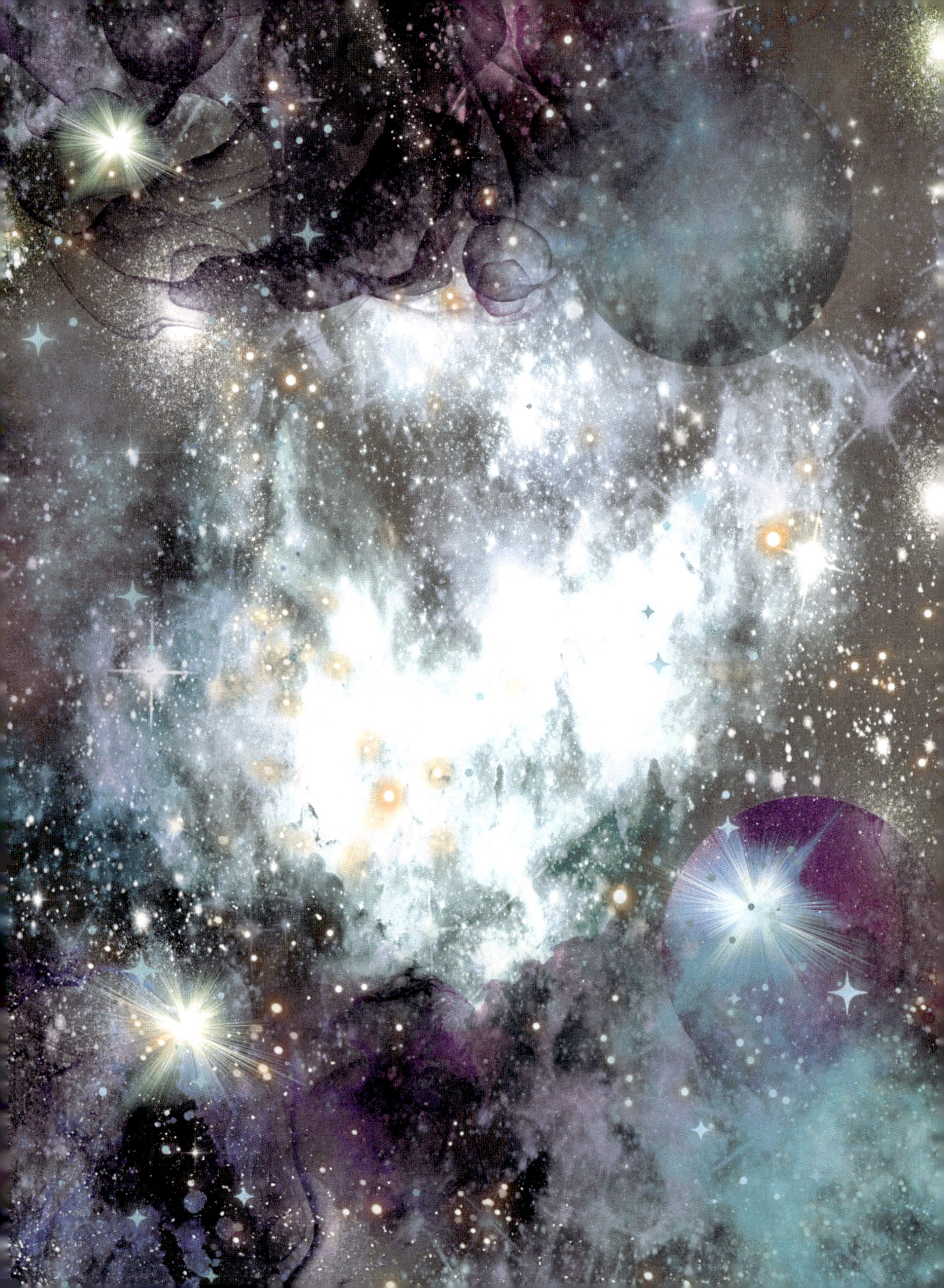

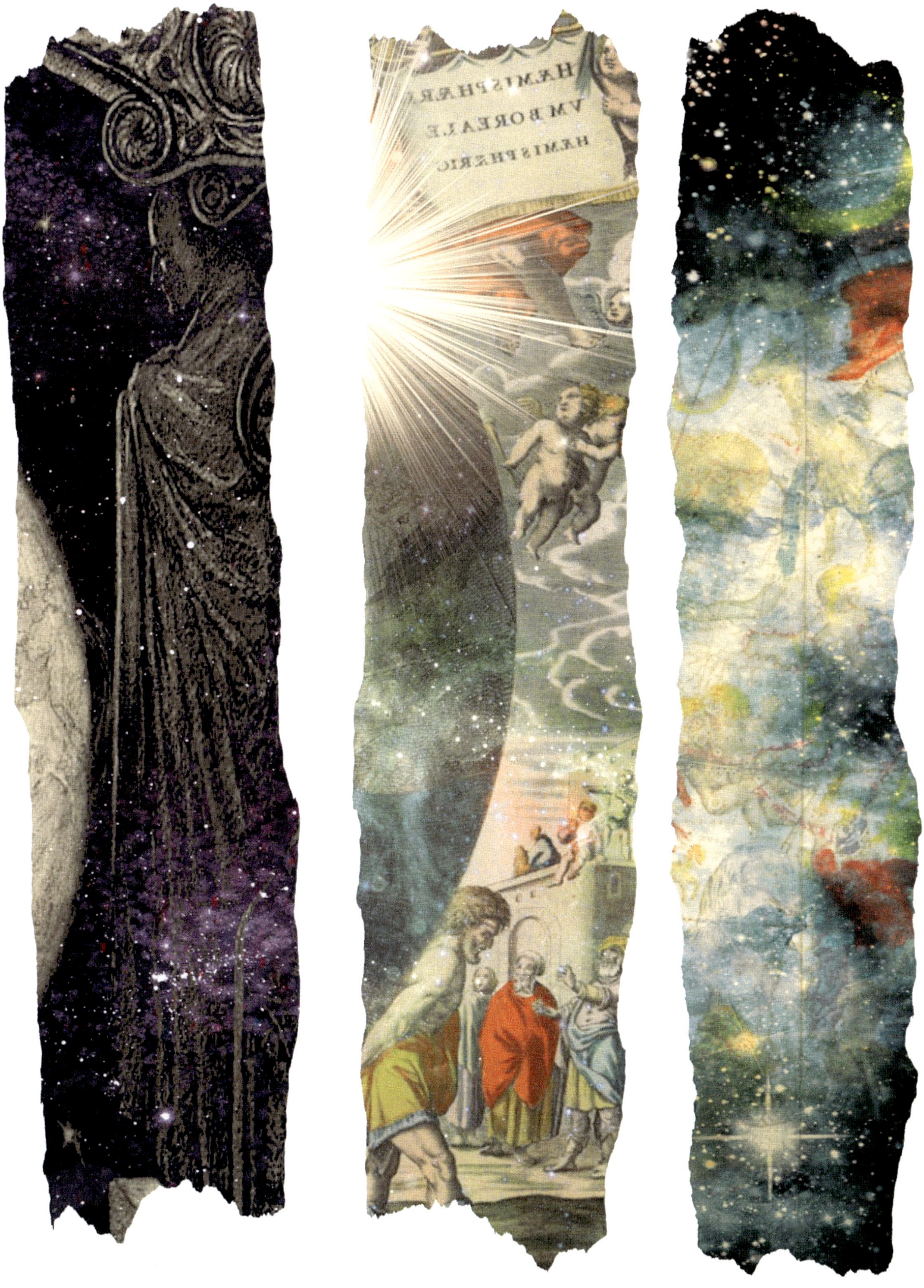